S0-CBA-550

Business Principles and Management

Eleventh Edition
Anniversary Edition
Volume 4

Kenneth E. Everard
James L. Burrow

COPYRIGHT © 2007 by Nelson, a division of Thomson Limited. Thomson Nelson is a registered trademark used herein under license.

Printed and bound in the United States of America

1 2 3 4 5 10 09 08 07

For more information contact Thomson Nelson
1120 Birchmount Road,
Scarborough, Ontario, M1K 5G4.
Or you can visit our internet site at
http://www.nelson.com

ALL RIGHTS RESERVED. No part of this work covered by the copyright hereon may be reproduced, transcribed, or used in any form or by any means – graphic, electronic, or mechanical, including photocopying, recording, taping, web distribution or information storage and retrieval systems – without the written permission of the publisher.

For permission to use material from this text or product, contact us by
Tel 1-800-730-2214
Fax 1-800-730-2215
www.thomsonrights.com

This textbook is a Nelson custom publication. Because your instructor has chosen to produce a custom publication, you pay only for material that you will use in your course.

Cover Photo: Stockbyte

ISBN-13: 978-0-17-646275-8
ISBN-10: 0-17-646275-9

Consists of:

Business Principles and Management, Eleventh Edition Anniversary Edition
Kenneth E. Everard
James L. Burrow
ISBN 0-538-43590-9, © 2004

Contents

· ·

· ·

UNIT SIX

PRODUCTION and MARKETING MANAGEMENT

CHAPTERS

514

It is the fate of most companies to see a competitor come out with something new that they should have thought of. Worse, the idea may have been kicking around in their organization without ever surfacing at a level where it could have been seized and launched. Good ideas are in the air, and what separates the masters from the plodders is how well organized they are to capture and evaluate ideas, and then to develop and launch them successfully.

Phillip Kotler
Kotler on Marketing, 1999

PRODUCT PLANNING AND PRODUCTION MANAGEMENT

OBJECTIVES

20-1 Discuss the steps in new product development.

20-2 Discuss the differences among manufacturing processes.

20-3 Describe several important considerations in locating a manufacturing business and organizing the production process.

20-4 Describe the ways businesses maintain product and service quality.

20-5 Identify the characteristics of services that make them different from products and the challenges service businesses face in meeting customer needs.

REALITY CHECK

ADVENTURES IN SHOPPING

aresa walked through the door of her home and collapsed on the couch. She and her friend, Desiree, had just returned from a shopping trip to a new store called Millennium. It was promoted as the "shopping experience for the 21st century," and the "alternative to the American mall." Although she was tired, she couldn't wait to tell her mother about the experience.

"It's the biggest store I've ever seen—bigger than the discount warehouses. The store seemed to have every product you could want and a lot of products I've never seen before."

Noticing how tired Laresa appeared, her mother asked, "With such a big store and so many products, do people really enjoy shopping there? I would think it would be confusing and exhausting."

Laresa replied, "It's really easy and fun. You don't have to walk. Instead, you can stand on slowly moving walkways just like you see in airports that move you up and down the aisles. There are huge video displays that identify the types of products in each area of the store as well as smaller computer screens you touch to find the products you want, see demonstrations of the products, and get answers to your questions. You don't have to carry any packages. If you see something you want to buy, you enter the information in the computer. They guarantee that if the product isn't in stock, it will be delivered to your home within 24 hours. All of your purchases are packaged and waiting for you when you're ready to leave. At the checkout, the clerk reviews your order, processes your payment, and even has the packages delivered to the curb so you can drive up with your car."

■ DEVELOPING NEW PRODUCTS

Laresa's experience demonstrates that businesses are constantly trying to find better ways to please customers. As consumers, we are offered a growing number of choices of products and services to satisfy our wants and needs. Businesses compete to develop and sell the products that consumers want. If consumers in Laresa's city decide that the new business offers them a better shopping experience, other stores will have to change in order to compete. As shown in Figure 20-1, before a business can offer new products to consumers, it must do the following:

1. Develop an idea for a new product that consumers want to buy.

2. Turn the idea into a workable product design.

3. Be able to produce the product and make it available to consumers at a price they are willing to pay.

If any one of the steps cannot be completed successfully, the product will fail.

Developing new products for sale is a very difficult and expensive task. For example, a national fast-food restaurant spent over a million dollars on research to develop a new sandwich for its menu. Then it spent additional millions of dollars developing a production process

FIGURE 20-1

The Steps in Product Development

1. **Develop an idea for a new product that customers want to buy.**
   - Conduct consumer research.
   - Conduct product research.
2. **Turn the idea into a workable product design.**
   - Build and test models of the product.
   - Determine what resources will be needed to produce large quantities of the product.
   - Determine the costs of producing the product and compare them to the product's price.
3. **Be able to produce the product and make it available to consumers at a price they are willing to pay.**
   - Build or remodel manufacturing facilities, if necessary.
   - Purchase raw materials.
   - Train employees.
   - Promote, distribute, and sell the product.

that would maintain a consistent taste and quality for the sandwich, no matter where the customer purchased it. In this case the sandwich was popular with consumers when it was introduced, so the company was able to recover all of its costs and make a profit. However, many times companies have spent that much money and more, only to find that not enough customers wanted the product. Their new product failed, and they lost all of the money they spent to develop it.

Only a small number of new product ideas ever reach the market. Even for those that do, over half will not survive in the market for five years. Therefore, a producer risks a large amount of money in buildings, equipment, materials, and personnel to provide the products that we consume.

Product development is the process of creating or improving a product or service. As a result of many factors, products are continuously changing—old products go out of use or are improved, and new products appear on the market. Most of the products you will be using in 10 years are not even available today. For a company to survive, it must continually search for ways to improve even its most successful products and regularly develop new products. Product development drives other business activities. Before a company can market, advertise, distribute, and sell a product, it must create and produce it. Think of the millions of dollars that were invested to develop the new store, Millennium, described at the beginning of the chapter. The investors in that business are excited by the new business idea, but to earn a return on their investment, the product must succeed.

■ CREATING PRODUCT IDEAS

The first step in product development is to come up with a good new product idea. You have probably seen a new product and said to yourself, "I could have thought of that." But developing successful product ideas is not easy. The process for coming up with the product ideas is both creative and scientific.

Ideas for new products can come from many sources. People inside and outside the company may suggest new product ideas. A company may get ideas from salespeople and production personnel, from other business people, and from research projects. Many companies employ people whose primary responsibility is to create and test new products.

CONSUMER RESEARCH Many companies gather information to help in product development by contacting the people who are likely to purchase the product. One of the best sources of ideas for product improvements or new products is a company's customers. They have used the company's products and know what they like and don't like, and what new products they would like to have. Companies can get this information from customers in many ways. Some companies send questionnaires to people who recently bought a product, asking for their opinions. Others have telephone numbers that customers can call or e-mail addresses they can use when they have questions or problems.

Salespeople can also gather information from customers. Since salespeople regularly talk to customers, they collect valuable information that can help the company improve its products. Managers should encourage salespeople to learn as much as they can about customer likes and dislikes. Many companies have specific procedures and forms

ILLUSTRATION 20-1

Why might a company use its customers to help in the process of product development?

FACTS AND FIGURES

J. D. Power and Associates is an internationally recognized marketing information firm. Automotive studies are the product for which the company is best known. These consumer opinion studies measure customer satisfaction from vehicle purchase through five years of ownership. Automobile manufacturers are provided with information resources that help them anticipate and respond to changes in the time-sensitive automobile industry.

for salespeople to use when they gather important information from customers. The procedures ensure that the information is communicated to the people responsible for product development.

If a company wants to get a great deal of information from consumers about possible new products, it might form a **consumer panel**—a group of people who offer opinions about a product or service. The panel consists of several people who have bought or are likely to buy the company's products. The panel members meet with trained interviewers to discuss their feelings about new products and to tell the representatives what they think the company can do to improve its current products.

Have you ever been shopping in a mall when someone asked you to participate in a short interview or product review? Companies often conduct research in places where customers shop. The research may involve asking customers a short series of questions about their experiences with products or a more complicated process in which consumers are shown samples of new products and asked detailed questions about them. The developers of Millennium, the large store described earlier that was so exciting to Laresa, likely used a great deal of consumer research to design the best combination of products, services, and store layout to meet customer needs.

PRODUCT RESEARCH Product research is research completed by engineers and other scientists to develop new products or to discover improvements for existing products. There are two types of product research—pure research and applied research. **Pure research** is research done without a specific product in mind. Researchers in many companies are continually searching for new processes, materials, or ideas. They are experts in specific areas, such as biology, chemistry, robotics, electronics, or energy sources. They conduct experiments and tests in order to make discoveries that might lead to new products.

Many products we use today have been developed as a result of such research. The latest computer technology, life-saving drugs, energy-efficient appliances and homes, and improved food products have resulted from pure research projects. Many of the products we consume have been changed and improved through chemical research. Some examples are low-calorie sweeteners, meat substitutes made from soybean products, and vitamin-enhanced soft drinks. Insulation used in beverage coolers and non-stick surfaces on cooking utensils and razor blades are products that have been developed through research conducted by scientists involved in the space program.

Universities, medical research facilities, and government-sponsored research programs are heavily involved in pure research. Because of those efforts, we will likely see products developed in the near future that use energy more efficiently, apply laser technology, provide more effective treatments for diseases, and result in improved prediction and control of the weather.

Applied research is research that studies existing product problems or possible design improvements for current products. Improvements in electric battery storage and the mechanics of engines are resulting in a new type of fuel-efficient automobile that combines a small combustion engine with a battery that can recharge while you drive. Fiber optics research continues to increase the amount of voice and data communications that can move on the same transmission line while maintaining security and quality. Digital video technology improves the quality of the images we see on our television and allows us to select from among hundreds of channels of information to develop a personal viewing package at any time of the day or night.

To be successful for a long time, products must be constantly changed and improved. Many types of improvements result from product research. Changes can be made in the physical product, or new features can be added to existing products. Researchers may discover new uses for the product or ways to make the product easier to use. Sometimes changes in the package itself—without actual product changes—can improve a product.

■ DESIGNING NEW PRODUCTS

In planning and producing a new product, businesses should involve all major departments, including production, finance, human resources, and marketing. The product should be designed to meet customer needs. Customers should be able to identify features of the new product that are different from and better than those of competing products. Also, products need to be safe and easy to use. They must meet all state and federal laws for product quality and environmental and consumer safety.

If research results in a new product idea that has a good chance for consumer acceptance, the company will begin to design the product. In this step, engineers and researchers build models of the product and test them to be sure that the company can design a quality product. The design process should include factors such as durability, ease of use, and a pleasing appearance. Usually a great deal of testing will occur to be sure the product will meet all requirements for success before the company will make the large investment needed to produce it.

Once a model has been built and tested, the company must determine what resources it will need to produce large quantities of the product. It may have to buy production facilities and equipment or modify those it is currently using to produce other products. If the company can use existing facilities and equipment, it must develop a production schedule that shows how it can produce the new products without disrupting the production of current products.

The company will have to determine the costs of producing the product and compare those costs to the price it will charge for the product. It is possible that the product cannot be sold at a price that will cover all of the research, design, and production costs. In this case, the company will decide not to produce the product. If the company can make the decision to halt development at this point, it will incur less financial loss than if it produces a large quantity that goes unsold or must be sold at a loss.

■ PRODUCING THE PRODUCT

If the new product has survived the research and design process, the company can begin producing for sale. This is an expensive step. The company may have to build or remodel its manufacturing facilities. It must purchase raw materials and hire and train enough employees to produce the product. Then it must promote, distribute, and sell the product. However, if the company has carefully planned and produced the product, the product has a better chance of succeeding and earning a profit for the company when customers purchase it.

As you learned in Chapter 1, *production* is making a product or providing a service. **Manufacturing** is a form of production in which raw and semifinished materials are processed, assembled, or converted into finished products.

Manufacturing is a complex process, even when only one product is produced. Examine any product you purchased recently. Very likely, it is made of several parts. The company must either manufacture those parts or purchase them from other companies. The manufacturer must store the parts until it needs them. Then people and machinery must assemble the parts. Once assembled, the product must be packaged. Many products will be packed together for shipping and then stored in a warehouse for delivery to the businesses that will sell them.

In addition to the activities just discussed, the manufacturing process involves many other tasks. The manufacturer must maintain equipment, purchase supplies, and train people to operate the equipment.

As you can see, manufacturing just one product is a complicated process. Often, manufacturers produce many products at the same time. So you can see how complicated it can be to operate a manufacturing business.

When you think of a manufacturing business, you may have an image of a large factory with a long assembly line. Workers perform specific activities on the assembly line as the product moves past. Many products, all looking exactly alike, are produced on the assembly line each day. But while assembly lines are one way to manufacture products, there are many other ways (see Figure 20-2).

MASS PRODUCTION   **Mass production** is an assembly process that produces a large number of identical products. It usually involves an assembly line where employees at each workstation continuously perform the same task to assemble the product. Many products you use are

TYPE OF MANUFACTURING	WHAT HAPPENS IN THE PROCESS
Mass Production	An assembly process produces a large number of identical products
Continuous Processing	Raw materials move through special equipment that changes their form to make them more usable for consumption or further manufacturing
Repetitive Production	The same thing is done over and over to produce a product
Intermittent Processing	Short production runs are used to make predetermined quantities of different products
Custom Manufacturing	A unique product is designed and built to meet the purchaser's specific needs

FIGURE 20-2

Different Types of Manufacturing

assembled through mass production. Automobiles, cameras, home appliances, and many brands of computers are mass-produced.

Mass production enables companies to manufacture products at a low cost and in large quantities. But many changes have occurred in mass production since Henry Ford first used assembly lines to produce cars in the early 1900s. Now, manufacturers often train assembly line workers to perform many activities. Workers can then switch tasks periodically to make the job more interesting. Teams of workers and supervisors meet regularly to identify problems and develop solutions. Computers monitor the assembly process to ensure that needed parts and materials are available at the right time and right place. Robots stationed at many places along assembly lines complete tasks such as painting, welding, and quality-control testing.

ILLUSTRATION 20-2

How has mass production changed since its first use in the early 1900s?

CONTINUOUS PROCESSING Raw materials usually need to be processed before they can be consumed. With **continuous processing,** raw materials constantly move through specially designed equipment that changes their form to make them more usable for consumption or further manufacturing. Steel mills, for example, convert iron ore into steel to be used by other manufacturers. Oil refineries change crude oil into a variety of petroleum products, including gasoline and oil. Cereal manufacturers process many different kinds of grain into the cereals you eat for breakfast. Production runs may last days, weeks, or months without equipment shutdowns.

REPETITIVE PRODUCTION Companies that use **repetitive production** do the same thing over and over to produce a product. The activity is usually rather simple and can be completed in a short time. The repetitive process may use modules (pre-assembled parts or units) in the assembly process. For example, the repetitive process is used to produce washing machines. First, the motor is assembled as a separate module. Then it is installed in the frame, which has been assembled separately. Controls, hoses, and other features may be added in yet another process. Mobile homes and recreational vehicles are often assembled using repetitive production. Individual sections are constructed and then brought together for final assembly on the frame or chassis.

INTERMITTENT PROCESSING **Intermittent processing** uses short production runs to make predetermined quantities of different products. The most common form of intermittent processing is the manufacturing or assembly of a specific product to meet a customer's order or specifications. An example of a business using intermittent manufacturing is a printing company. Each printing job varies in quantity, type of printing process, binding, color of ink, and type of paper. When the company receives an order, the printer assigned to the job assembles the necessary materials, selects the correct printing equipment, and completes the printing. A bakery uses intermittent processing, as does a company that roasts, blends, and grinds many varieties of coffee beans to order.

CUSTOM MANUFACTURING Often there is a need to build only one or a very limited number of units of a product. The product may be very large or complex and take a long time to build. **Custom manufacturing** is the process used to design and build a unique product to meet the specific needs of the purchaser. Buildings, bridges, and computer programs are all examples of custom manufacturing. If a company needs a special piece of equipment built, it hires a custom manufacturer.

A custom manufacturer must be able to work with a customer to develop a unique product. The company must be flexible enough to build a different product each time, and it may need to build part or all of that product at a new location each time.

■ PLANNING A MANUFACTURING BUSINESS

Establishing a manufacturing business requires a number of important decisions. The company must be able to get the materials it needs to build products. It must have buildings designed and built. The company must purchase specialized machinery and equipment and arrange it in the buildings so that it can produce quality products rapidly and at a low cost. The company must hire people with the skills to perform the many activities needed to produce the products. If it cannot find people with the needed skills, it must train others. Finally, after manufacturing the products, the company must store them until it can sell and distribute them to customers.

■ LOCATING THE BUSINESS

One of the first decisions of the manufacturing company is where to locate the business. While it might seem that a business could locate anywhere it wants to, it is a very complicated procedure to find the best location. As illustrated in Figure 20-3, several factors influence the decision of where to locate a manufacturing business.

AVAILABILITY OF RAW MATERIALS If a manufacturer needs to process raw materials as a part of the production process, it must have a reliable supply of those materials. Also, the cost of the raw materials must be as low as possible. The manufacturer, therefore, may choose to locate close to the source of the raw materials to make them easier to obtain and to keep the cost of transporting them as low as possible. Furniture and textile manufacturers, steel mills, and food-processing companies are examples of industries that locate close to the source of needed raw materials. Consider what the most important raw mate-

Availability of Raw Materials

Transportation Methods

Supply and Cost of Energy and Water

Land and Building Costs

Labor Supply

Location of Customers

Economic and Legal Factors

FIGURE 20-3

The Factors in Deciding a Manufacturing Facility's Location

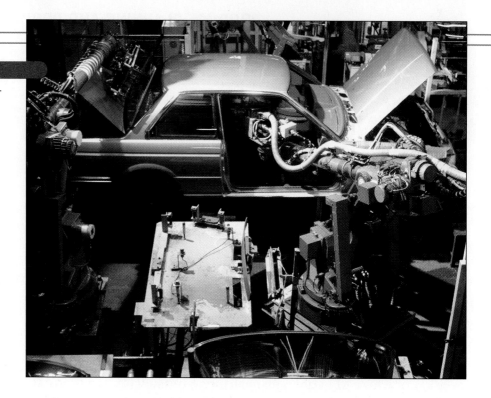

rials are for each of these manufacturers and where the manufacturers are likely to locate because of the need for these materials.

TRANSPORTATION METHODS The company must decide how to obtain the materials needed to manufacture the products and how it will ship the products to customers. The choice of transportation method can determine whether the company will receive materials and deliver products on time. The major transportation methods include air, rail, truck, water, and pipeline. Each has specific advantages based on time, cost, and convenience. Very bulky, fragile, or perishable products will need special transportation. Companies may decide to locate close to a railroad, an interstate highway system, or a major airport to be able to conveniently access the type of transportation needed. If the company is involved in international business, it may need to locate near a variety of transportation sources.

SUPPLY AND COST OF ENERGY AND WATER The costs and supply of energy that manufacturers use is an important consideration in production planning. The company must have an uninterrupted supply of energy (such as electricity, gasoline, or coal) at a reasonable cost. There have been times in recent years when several types of energy, including electricity and gasoline, have been in short supply. As a result, companies had to switch to other forms of energy or reduce operations. Energy prices can change dramatically in a short time, making it difficult to control costs. Water supplies are limited in many parts of the United States as well as in other countries. Governments tightly control access to water as well as the requirements for treatment and discharge of wastewater. Cities and states have passed environmental laws that regulate access to water and energy resources and where specific types of businesses can and cannot locate. A company must be sure to locate where it will have enough energy and water to be able to operate for many years in the future.

LAND AND BUILDING COSTS While some companies can operate in small buildings, others may need several hundred acres of land. Companies can purchase or lease land and buildings. Constructing a large manufacturing building will cost many millions of dollars. A company will need a source of financing for the construction and will normally pay the cost of the building over many years.

As a business grows, it must plan for possible future expansion. Many companies have had to expand several times since they started business. Expansion is easier if enough land is available close to the existing buildings, and buildings are designed to be flexible and allow for expansion.

Companies must carefully consider how the manufacturing process will affect other people and organizations located in the same area. Businesses with production processes that create odors or high noise levels may be severely restricted in where they can locate or may face lawsuits from adjoining neighborhoods.

LABOR SUPPLY Well-trained employees are an important part of most manufacturing operations. In selecting a location, a company should look at the available supply of workers, the training they might need, and the cost of the labor. The choice of location depends on whether the company needs highly skilled employees or unskilled labor. Few businesses can operate effectively today without well-educated employees. The days of easily available and inexpensive labor providing the skills a company needs are over. Businesses are working with government agencies, colleges, and universities to design training programs, so they will have a competitive workforce.

CYBER COMMUNICATION

E-mail is so easy to use that employees can be lulled into a false sense of security that results in the sending of overly blunt, abrupt, explicit, or careless messages. Although there are laws forbidding people to read others' postal mail, electronic mail has no such protection. In fact, an employee's e-mail is considered the property of the organization. As a result, businesses worried about lawsuits are using sophisticated tools to monitor employee e-mail. That, in turn, is raising concerns about the proper balance between employees' privacy and the employer's need to know.

Some privacy experts believe that private, interpersonal communication is an important human function in the workplace. Employees should be allowed to use e-mail without worrying about reprisals. However, some businesses fear complaints of computer harassment and possible lawsuits.

Businesses have responded to the problem in a variety of ways. Some say they limit monitoring to incidents when there is suspicion of wrongdoing. Other organizations warn employees each time they sign on that their e-mail isn't private. Meanwhile, the standard advice is for employees not to e-mail anything they wouldn't want to see on a company bulletin board with their signature.

ACTIVITY Conduct a debate in class on which is more important—employees' privacy or the employer's need to know. What arguments can be made in favor of and against each point of view?

LOCATION OF CUSTOMERS Just as some companies need to locate near the source of raw materials, others may consider the location of their customers. This is an important factor when most of the customers can be found in one part of the country, when they need products regularly and rapidly, or when transportation costs of the finished products will be very high.

Manufacturers that supply parts for the auto industry usually locate near the automobile production facilities. Some companies locate near seaports if they have important markets in other countries. Since soft drink companies must provide a regular, fresh supply of their product to many stores and businesses, they have bottling plants and distribution centers in most cities to reduce transportation costs.

Today some states are developing large airfreight centers. These are airports that are surrounded by efficient distribution centers and with easy access to interstate highways and rail lines. The airfreight centers are being created to attract to those locations manufacturing businesses that need to ship products quickly by air.

ECONOMIC AND LEGAL FACTORS A company also considers the type and amount of taxes it must pay in the location of its manufacturing facilities. Some cities offer reduced tax rates or may even remove some taxes for several years to encourage new businesses to locate there. Others have taxes on inventory and equipment that increase the costs of business operations. Most towns and cities use zoning laws to restrict where businesses can locate and how they can operate. Environmental regulations control the use of water and energy as well as require businesses to avoid polluting the water, air, and land.

■ PRODUCTION PLANNING

Developing a production plan can be compared to planning a meal. All ingredients must be available in the right quantities and at the right time. Cooking utensils need to be assembled. Since some foods require longer cooking times than others, preparation of each item must begin at the correct time. If scheduled and completed correctly, all foods can be served at the same time.

When planning production, the company identifies all of the resources required to produce the product and estimates when each will be needed and in what quantity. Because production occurs over a period of time and in a sequence, the company will not need all resources at once. If the company receives the materials before it needs them, it will have to use both space and money for storage. On the other hand, if the company can't get the resources when needed, it will have to delay production and spend money for employee time and materials that it can't use until the necessary materials arrive.

Three important activities are a part of production planning. **Inventory management** is planning the quantities of materials and supplies needed for production and the amount of finished products required to meet customer orders. **Human resource planning** is determining the types of jobs required for each part of production, the number of people needed for each job, and the skills each person will need in order to do the job. **Production scheduling** is identifying the steps required in a manufacturing process, the time required to complete each step, and the sequence of the steps. Managers use sophisticated planning systems to help them develop production schedules. Computers are very useful in scheduling production and monitoring progress toward meeting production schedules.

■ BUILDING LAYOUT

A manufacturer must organize its facilities, equipment, and materials to produce products efficiently. Products have to move through the building, parts must be added, and employees must be able to work on the product easily and safely. The manufacturer must have cost-effective methods for receiving and storing raw materials, parts, and supplies. Once products are finished, the manufacturer must store them or load them for shipment.

The type of layout a manufacturer uses will depend on the product and the assembly process. For example, one company that builds tractors has a continuous assembly line that is nearly a mile long. Many of the parts have to be stored long distances from the place they are needed. The parts are delivered to the assembly line with overhead conveyor belts and chains.

A small company that builds electric motors delivers all needed parts to each assembler's work area. The assembler puts the parts together to finish the motor. The motor then moves to the shipping area for packaging and storing for delivery.

A company that manufacturers desktop computers organizes its manufacturing employees in teams with their own work area. Each team orders the parts it needs and keeps them in easy-to-reach bins around its workspace. Then the entire team works on the assembly, tests the computer to be sure it works, and packages it for delivery. This procedure allows the company to quickly build a customized computer for each customer's order.

In addition to the type of product and the assembly process used, other factors influence the layout of the business. The layout should be designed to make product assembly easy and safe. Employees may need areas to test and repair products. Products and people must be able to move around the building. They will need food services and break areas. Other activities that support the manufacturing process, such as purchasing, information management, training, and administrative services, need space to work.

For most companies, the layout should be flexible so they can add new machinery and equipment. Also, companies may need to expand the layout as the company grows or change it to produce new products.

■ IMPROVING PRODUCTION PROCESSES

Improving quality and productivity has been one of the most important challenges facing businesses in the last decade. Increasing global competition has resulted in a larger number of products from which customers can choose. Businesses have found that customers will buy the best product available for the price they can afford, resulting in increased pressure to improve quality while holding down costs and prices.

As you learned in Chapter 1, for many years companies were more interested in production efficiency than in quality. As early as the 1950s, Dr. W. Edwards Deming was encouraging businesses to focus on quality as the most important company goal, but his ideas were largely ignored in the United States. However, because of the success of companies that have adopted Deming's ideas, most manufacturers use principles of quality management today. **Quality management** is a process for assuring product quality by developing standards for all operations and products and measuring results against those standards. For quality management to succeed, the company must believe that no defects are acceptable and that all employees are responsible for quality. Everyone must be able to identify problems and take responsibility for correcting them. Rewards need to be based on achieving the quality standards rather than meeting a certain level of production.

To encourage American companies to improve quality, Congress created the Malcolm Baldrige National Quality Award in 1987. To win the award, a company must demonstrate that it has implemented a program to develop and maintain quality in all of its products and activities. Companies compete for the award because customers are more likely to buy from companies that can prove their commitment to quality by winning this honor.

Technology has contributed to the improvement of manufacturing for many years. Computers have dramatically improved the quality and speed of production and have reduced costs. Robots now complete many of the routine and repetitive tasks previously done by low-skilled employees.

Exam ¹ —
? 8

ILLUSTRATION 20-4

Technology has greatly contributed to the improvement of manufacturing. What effect have computers had on the employees of such companies?

GLOBAL PERSPECTIVE

ISO PROMOTES GLOBAL QUALITY

Global trade has created a variety of problems for companies, along with the opportunities to reach new customers with their products and services. One of the greatest challenges has been the lack of standardization among the products produced by different companies. Consider the problems that a company creates when it produces machinery that cannot be sold in another country because it is not compatible with the machinery that customers in that country already use. What if a company needs to make repairs and the available parts don't match the broken parts?

The International Organization for Standardization (ISO) was organized to deal with the standardization issue, which is a barrier to international trade. The two primary goals of this international organization are:

- to develop agreements on production designs to increase compatibility among products that are used with each other, and
- to establish standards to ensure quality and reliability when one company purchases the products of another company.

Over 130 countries participate in the voluntary organization. Because of the agreements developed by the ISO, products such as credit cards can be used in cash machines in any country and batteries produced in one country will work in a CD player produced in another country. If an airline needs to replace a bolt in an engine mount while the plane is in another country, it can be assured that the bolt produced in that country will fit.

Standards known as ISO 9000 establish very specific requirements for manufacturing processes and product specifications. Any business that works with another ISO-certified business can trust that the requirements have been met. A newer set of standards, ISO 14000, describes specific requirements for environmental management. A company that agrees to these standards assures that it will follow rigorous guidelines in the use of resources and protection of the environment.

Many government agencies and individual companies will not purchase products from a company that is not ISO certified. Companies spend a great deal of time and undertake expensive training programs to make sure that their products and processes meet the ISO requirements. The result is much more efficient trade among businesses and countries, plus increasing quality of products and operations in thousands of companies.

The International Organization for Standardization has had a big impact on the ways businesses interact with each other. It continues its work as new technologies emerge and as manufacturing problems are identified to make the process of international trade easier.

THINK CRITICALLY

1. What are some examples of products that are not standardized, resulting in problems using one brand with another?
2. Why would a company refuse to work with other companies that are not ISO certified?
3. Why might a company decide not to meet the standards established by ISO?
4. Use the Internet to locate companies that identify themselves as ISO certified. Find Web sites that provide additional information or that describe specific ISO standards.

Fewer people are now needed to accomplish the same level of production. However, the people needed must be skilled in computer operations and modern production processes.

In addition to routine tasks, computer technology can also accomplish very difficult and challenging tasks. Using a computer application known as **computer-aided design (CAD),** engineers can design and test products before they are even built. With a computer, engineers can view a design from various angles, study possible modifications, and test the products for strength and durability.

The most extensive use of computers in manufacturing is a system known as **computer-integrated manufacturing.** With this process, all manufacturing systems are designed and managed using computers. Design work, planning and scheduling, resource management, and control are all tied together through computers. When someone makes a change in one area, computers determine the impact of the change on other areas and communicate that information to the affected work units.

The Internet has now become a powerful resource in improving the speed and quality of manufacturing. Some of the uses of the Internet are very basic but have an amazing impact on how a business operates. As an example, it used to be a very expensive and time-consuming process for companies to get approval from the Food and Drug Administration in Washington, D.C., when they wanted to produce a new food product or drug. They had already spent months and often years developing and testing the product. Then they had to prepare, print, and ship volumes of reports to the FDA for approval. Today that entire process can be managed on the Web. Companies can transmit reports instantly, research questions online, send answers to the FDA by e-mail, and conduct meetings on computer screens. The time for obtaining approval has been cut in half, and the cost of approval has gone down substantially.

An automobile manufacturer with plants in many countries around the world is improving the automobile design process using the Internet. Product designers come together in cyberspace to share ideas and plan new products. If one factory identifies design or manufacturing problems, it can immediately share information about the problem with every other facility and cooperatively develop a solution. The system is resulting in cost savings because there are fewer design problems and good designs are now being used over and over in many locations. Also, the manufacturer benefits from greater creativity in developing new automobile models as people from around the world share their ideas.

■ SERVICE BUSINESSES

Service businesses are the fastest growing segment of our society. Over two thirds of the U.S. labor force are now employed in service-producing businesses or service jobs. Over half of our consumer purchases are services. Therefore, the U.S. is changing from the world's

FACTS AND FIGURES

E-commerce is creating new pressures on manufacturers for quicker response and shorter cycle times. "Lean manufacturing" is aimed at the elimination of waste in every area of production, including customer relations, product design, supplier networks, and factory management. Its goal is to incorporate less human effort, less inventory, and less time to develop products—while producing top-quality products in the most efficient and economical manner possible.

leading manufacturing economy into its leading service economy. While many service businesses are quite small and employ only a few people, others have total sales of millions of dollars each year and employ thousands of people.

■ NATURE OF SERVICES

Figure 20-4 illustrates that services are very different from products. As you learned in Chapter 1, *services* are activities of value that do not result in the ownership of anything tangible. Traditional service businesses include theaters, travel agencies, beauty and barbershops, lawn care businesses, and insurance agencies. New types of services are emerging as well, such as Internet service providers (ISPs) that connect you to the Internet, comprehensive financial services providers, and companies that provide information management or human resource management services for other companies. Services have important characteristics that make them different from products. These differences in form, availability, quality, and timing result in unique operating procedures for service businesses.

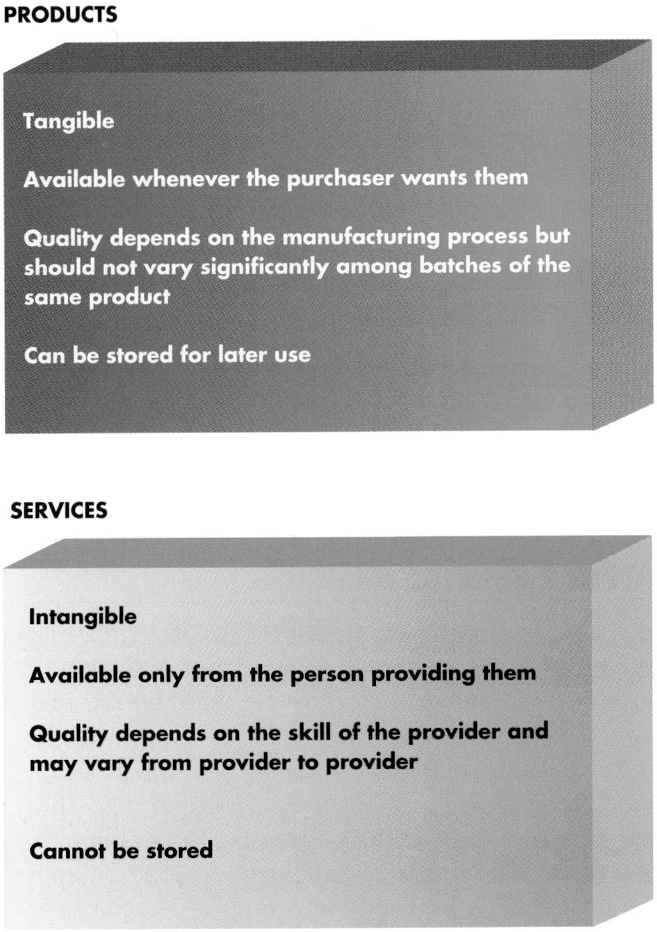

Exam?
? 14

PRODUCTS

Tangible

Available whenever the purchaser wants them

Quality depends on the manufacturing process but should not vary significantly among batches of the same product

Can be stored for later use

SERVICES

Intangible

Available only from the person providing them

Quality depends on the skill of the provider and may vary from provider to provider

Cannot be stored

FIGURE 20-4

The Differences Between Products and Services

FORM Services are intangible. They do not include a physical product, they cannot be seen or examined before purchase, and they do not exist after the consumer uses them. When you go to a theater to see a play, you rely on a review in the newspaper or what you have heard from others to decide if it is something you want to attend. If a company hires a carpet cleaning business for its offices, it will need to bring them back again when the carpets must be cleaned again.

AVAILABILITY The service cannot be separated from the person or business supplying it. Dental care requires a dentist, a concert requires an orchestra, and tax preparation advice requires an accountant. People who purchase services are also purchasing the availability and the skill of the person performing the service. If a business or individual is unable to deliver a service, customers must go without. Trading in the stock market using the Internet has become popular as investors bypass traditional stockbrokers. However, in several instances, the business offering Internet stock trading had serious hardware or software problems that prevented customers from accessing accounts to buy and sell stocks.

QUALITY The quality of the service depends on who provides it as well as on where and when that service is provided. Removing 10 inches of snow from a parking lot may be more effective with a tractor and a dump truck than with a small snow blower. A hairstylist who has not completed training recently may not be able to offer the latest hair designs. Knowing these factors makes it much easier for a business to control the quality of services and ensure that customers get the same quality time after time. A service provider who is tired, untrained, or unconcerned about the customer may not provide the same quality of service each time.

TIMING A service cannot be stored or held until needed. After a movie starts, it is no longer available in its complete form until it is replayed. If the courts in a tennis club are full, no one else can play tennis at that time. Likewise, the owner of a taxi company must have cars and drivers available, even if no one is using a taxi at a specific time.

■ OPERATING A SERVICE BUSINESS

By understanding the unique characteristics of services, managers in charge of planning services can do a better job of meeting customer needs. Consider the planning that must be done by the managers of Millennium, the new store described at the beginning of the chapter. The store must make sure the business offers the best level of customer service possible to the thousands of people who shop there.

Because a service is intangible, service providers must find ways to describe their service to prospective customers. They may have to demonstrate how they will provide the service and the benefits the

FACTS AND FIGURES

The Ritz-Carlton Hotel Company is the only two-time recipient of the Malcolm Baldrige National Quality Award in the service category. The Ritz-Carlton's strategy is to achieve 100 percent customer loyalty. The company set a target of "defect-free" experiences for guests, implementing a measurement system to chart progress toward elimination of all customer problems—no matter how minor. Any employee can spend up to $2,000 to immediately correct a problem or handle a complaint.

customers will receive. To help overcome this problem, service businesses sometimes provide a product to customers as part of the service. Insurance companies provide policy documents and leather cases to hold the documents, tour services provide travel bags, and hotels provide small gifts in their rooms to remind their guests of the service and the service provider.

ILLUSTRATION 20-5

How can employees of service businesses do a better job of meeting customers' needs?

The service must be available and must be provided in an acceptable way to the customer. A client visiting a barbershop may want the services of a specific barber. A person completing a banking transaction may want to talk with a teller rather than use an ATM. Airline travelers may prefer not to stand in long lines to check their luggage and get a boarding pass for their flight.

The people providing the service must be well trained. They must be able to work with customers, identify needs, and provide the appropriate service. They must recognize that customer satisfaction is directly related to how well they perform. In turn, customers will expect the same quality of service each time they purchase it.

The supply of a service must be matched to the demand. If a bus company expects a large number of customers to ride its buses on the Saturday of a home football game, it may have to schedule more buses. If a snowstorm is anticipated, companies that clear parking lots and driveways may need to find additional equipment and operators. During a particularly cool and rainy summer, the operator of a swimming pool will probably need to schedule fewer lifeguards and pool attendants.

CHANGES IN SERVICE BUSINESSES

Just as manufacturers are constantly improving their products and processes to better satisfy customers, service businesses also look for better ways to provide services. Some of those ways include more careful hiring and training of employees, thoroughly planning how to maintain service quality standards, and using technology to improve the delivery and availability of services. The Internet is providing both opportunities and challenges for service businesses. For example, it is easier to get information to customers using the Internet. Pizzas, CDs, and videotapes can now be ordered online. However, when customers can download movies via the Internet or can place grocery orders at their favorite supermarket and have products delivered to their door, traditional businesses must consider the potential impact on their sales and profits.

Franchises for service businesses are becoming quite common. Franchising allows a service to be provided in a variety of locations while maintaining a consistent image and level of quality. Examples of franchised service businesses include car repair, video rentals, tax preparation and legal services, and house-cleaning businesses.

Service businesses are responding to the specific needs of customers. Extended hours, more service locations, a greater variety of services, and follow-up activities with customers to ensure satisfaction are all ways that businesses are attempting to meet customer needs. Managers of service businesses are learning that they must plan their service processes as carefully as manufacturers plan their processes. In both cases, customers expect a quality product or service delivered in a timely fashion at a fair price.

CHAPTER CONCEPTS

■ Businesses are continually looking for new product ideas and ways to improve their current products. Only products that meet consumer needs are likely to succeed.

■ Businesses use research to develop ideas for new products. Consumer research involves prospective and current customers in determining what new products and product improvements they prefer. Product research is done by scientists and engineers to discover new products and product improvements.

■ The design process for new products begins with building and testing a model to be sure the company can manufacture a product that meets consumer needs and that will be safe and durable. Then the company determines the resources and facilities necessary to produce large quantities of the new product. Finally, the company decides if it can produce and sell the product profitably.

■ Companies use different manufacturing processes, depending on the type of product and the needs of customers. Those processes include mass production, continuous processing, repetitive production, intermittent processing, and custom manufacturing.

■ When deciding where to put their facilities, manufacturers consider the location and availability of raw materials, transportation methods, and supplies of energy and water. They also consider the costs of land and buildings, the labor supply, the location of customers, and any economic and legal factors affecting the business.

■ Production planning involves three important activities—inventory management, human resource planning, and production scheduling. Also, the manufacturing facility should be designed to make production efficient, safe, and appropriate for the type of products and the production process to be used. Technology has influenced the way companies plan products and manage production.

■ Service businesses are now the fastest growing segment of our economy. The characteristics of services that make them different from products are their form, availability, quality, and timing.

BUILD VOCABULARY POWER

Define the following terms and concepts.

1. product development
2. consumer panel
3. product research
4. pure research
5. applied research
6. manufacturing
7. mass production
8. continuous processing
9. repetitive production
10. intermittent processing
11. custom manufacturing
12. inventory management
13. human resource planning
14. production scheduling
15. quality management
16. computer-aided design (CAD)
17. computer-integrated manufacturing

REVIEW FACTS

1. What are the three steps a business must follow before it can offer new products to consumers?
2. Why are customers a useful source of information for new products or product improvements?
3. How is pure research different from applied research?
4. Why should a company produce a model of a new product before it begins to produce large quantities of the product?
5. What should a company do if it finds that it can't sell a new product at a price that will cover all of its costs?
6. What is the difference between mass production and continuous processing?
7. Why should some businesses locate close to sources of raw materials while others should locate close to their customers?
8. What economic and legal factors might affect the location of a manufacturing business?
9. How is production planning similar to planning a meal?
10. What are three tools that can be used to improve production management?
11. Why do companies compete for the Malcolm Baldrige Award?
12. Give four examples of service businesses.
13. What four characteristics make services different from products?
14. Why is employee selection and training so important to a service business?
15. In what ways has the Internet affected the operations of service businesses?

DISCUSS IDEAS

1. Why should a company use both consumer research and product research when developing new product ideas?
2. What are some benefits and limitations of using research to develop products?
3. Why would a company invest money in pure research rather than applied research?
4. What are some methods used by product developers to collect data for research? How might technology be used in research?
5. Under what circumstances might a company decide to go ahead with the production of a new product rather than spend time developing and testing a model?
6. Use the Business section of a telephone directory, an Internet business directory, or another source to identify businesses that use each of the four types of manufacturing processes.
7. Of the factors that manufacturers consider in locating their facilities, which is most and least important in your opinion? Why?
8. Identify several ways that computers can be used to improve the manufacturing process.

9. Why are the number and size of service businesses increasing in the U.S. economy?

10. How does the concept of production scheduling apply to a service business?

11. How do you believe the Internet will affect the design and delivery of products and services in the next decade?

ANALYZE INFORMATION

1. The Neveau Corporation spent $8,937,250 on research last year. It spent 30 percent on consumer research, 25 percent on pure research, and the remainder on applied research. The company's annual sales for the last year were $297,550,000.

   a. What percentage of sales did the company spend on research?

   b. How much did the company spend on each of the three types of research?

2. A club you belong to has decided to prepare Valentine's Day baskets to sell in school as a fundraiser. The following items will make up the Valentine gift:

   ■ Small basket
   ■ Tissue paper for lining the basket
   ■ Fabric ribbon for bows
   ■ Three types of candies
   ■ Small artificial roses
   ■ "Be my Valentine" stickers
   ■ Personalized note card

   You plan to assemble the baskets on the afternoon of February 13th so they can be available for sale on the morning of the 14th. You will need to assemble 200 baskets.

   Using your classroom as the space for production, develop a plan for mass production of the Valentine's baskets. Complete a drawing that illustrates the assembly process. Make sure to allow space for the component parts while the baskets are being assembled and for the assembled baskets when they are completed. Consider how you will make the assembly process efficient and how you will ensure a quality product.

3. Participate in a debate with other students in your class. Your teacher will provide instructions on how the debate will be organized. Use research to gather information in support of your position. The two positions to be debated are:

   a. Cities and states should encourage economic development and provide better jobs for their citizens by reducing the amount of regulation on where manufacturing businesses can locate.

   b. Cities and states should increase the regulation of where businesses can locate to protect the environment and its citizens.

4. Join a team with several other students in your class. Your teacher may assign you to a specific group and topic. Use an Internet browser to gather information on one of the following topics: Dr. W. Edwards Deming; Malcolm Baldrige National Quality Award; ISO; Total Quality Management; Continuous Quality Improvement. Prepare an oral report. Include slides developed with computer presentation software. Provide at least three Internet addresses (URLs) where you found useful information on the topic.

5. Develop a chart that lists across the top the four characteristics of services that make them different from products. Then list five service businesses with which you are familiar in the left-hand column of the chart. Now complete the chart by describing how each business provides each of the characteristics listed.

SOLVE BUSINESS PROBLEMS

CASE 20-1

TaeMark, a major software development company, is facing increasing competition from many new businesses. It prides itself on staying in touch with its customers and carefully testing all new software products and upgrades to insure that they are easy to use and free of "bugs" before distributing them for sale. That process is both time-consuming and expensive. It often takes more than a year to get a new type of software on the market. The cost of the research and testing makes the company's software among the most expensive on the market.

TaeMark has noticed a new trend in software development in the past several years. Small and large competitors are flooding the market with new software. Many of the new products never achieve a high level of sales and often are removed from the market after a few months. However, it appears the competitors are willing to develop many products that don't sell with the hope that a few will be very successful and profitable. Also, most of the new software products are introduced without much testing to ensure quality. The new software developers believe that customers will put up with problems as long as the company quickly puts out a new edition of the software that corrects the problem. Competitors may put out two or three editions of a product in the time it takes TaeMark to develop and test one product. Because of the way the new software developers operate, they can price their software much lower than TaeMark can. TaeMark is also finding a change in customer attitudes about software developers. Customers express growing dissatisfaction with quality and say they are not willing to pay high prices for software when they know they will have to upgrade the software frequently.

Think Critically:

1. Why do you believe some companies are willing to forego the time and cost of research and testing in order to get products on the market faster?

2. Why do you believe customers appear to have negative attitudes toward software developers yet are still willing to purchase their products?

3. The new competitors are allowing customers to identify problems with their software. Then, they develop new editions that correct the problems. Is this really a form of research? Why or why not?

4. Would you advise TaeMark to change its product development process to be more like the new competitors or to continue the process it has used in the past? What are the advantages and disadvantages of each choice?

CASE 20-2

Rebecca and Jacob DeNucci vacation with their family each summer on an island just off the coast of North Carolina. The island is a popular tourist area with several large hotels and a ferry boat that brings people from the mainland to the island for day-long visits. Rebecca and Jacob began to think about ways they could use their time to make money during the summer. They thought about the needs of the tourists visiting the island, and they decided to begin a guide service for those people who wanted to explore the hills and forests of the island.

They spent some time planning two different tours. The short tour would last one hour. It would be for those people who wanted to see some of the beautiful spots on the island but were not prepared for extensive hiking. The long tour would take a half day and would include hiking over five miles. It was designed for the more experienced outdoors person who wanted to study the plants, trees, and wildlife unique to the island. They would provide the short tour to groups of 10 to 15 people at a rate of $2.00 per person. The long tour would serve four to eight people and would cost $10.00 per person.

After planning, Rebecca and Jacob developed small posters and some business cards that described their guide service, listed the days and hours the tours were available, and gave their home phone number. They distributed their materials to the hotels and restaurants on the island and the mainland.

Think Critically:

1. Do you think Rebecca and Jacob have done effective planning for their service business? What are some additional things they may want to consider before beginning the business?

2. Suggest ways that the DeNuccis can (a) help prospective customers understand the type and quality of their service, (b) ensure that customers get a high-quality service each time, and (c) provide the service to customers at an appropriate time and location.

3. During the second summer, the DeNuccis' business became extremely successful, and more tours were requested than they could personally lead. Now they are considering hiring other teenagers who also vacation on the island to lead the tours. What recommendations would you make on the qualifications and training of the new employees?

PROJECT: MY BUSINESS, INC.

Two important elements of product planning for a new retail business are (1) gathering information from potential customers about their attitudes toward the product and (2) scheduling the activities to be completed in organizing the business. You will complete those two activities in this section of the project.

DATA COLLECTION

1. Identify five people who represent potential customers for your business. They are your consumer panel, so select people who represent different ages, income levels, occupations, and interests. If possible, meet with them as a group. If that is not possible, then meet with each one individually. During the meeting, describe your business idea to them and provide them with a survey that asks for their reactions. Have them recommend what they would like to see in the products, prices, and location. They might also recommend some effective ways to promote the business. After you have met with the panel, write a report that summarizes its recommendations.

2. Identify and complete a detailed analysis of as many different juice drinks and related products as you can find in the town or city in which you live. For those that seem to be most popular, try to identify what product features (including factors such as the package) make them successful. Also identify any product features that you believe should be improved. Prepare a survey questionnaire to test your analysis of the product features. Your goal is to find out what features your customers really want. Ask at least ten people (who are not classmates) to complete your survey.

ANALYSIS

1. Prepare a written analysis of the recommendations you collected from your consumer panel. Select the recommendations that you would implement and give your reasons.
2. Prepare a written analysis of the data you collected from your product survey. Summarize your conclusions about what product features your customers want.

3. Search the Internet to find a list of the recommended steps for opening a new business. Then develop a schedule that lists the activities in the order that you would complete them for your business. Prepare a time schedule for the completion of each activity. Make certain you allow enough time to complete each activity. Project the date you will be able to open your business.
4. Since your juice business relies on effective service, prepare a list of services you will provide to customers. Then prepare a step-by-step procedure for each service to ensure quality of service delivery each time.

NATURE AND SCOPE OF MARKETING

OBJECTIVES

21-1 Discuss the importance of marketing and its role in the economy.

21-2 List the activities that are a part of marketing.

21-3 Define basic marketing concepts and the four elements of the marketing mix.

21-4 Explain the four stages of the product life cycle.

21-5 Identify the consumer goods classifications.

REALITY CHECK

THE SUPPLY VS. DEMAND DILEMMA

ony Taylor looked back on the past week with amazement. He remembered that on Monday he sat through his economics class learning about the concept of supply and demand. As he listened, he thought, "This doesn't apply to me. At most, it might affect some very large businesses. I wonder why we're studying it." But what a week!

He and three friends had wanted to see a certain movie for several weeks but could not find a time when they could all go together. Finally, everyone was available after school on Tuesday to catch the 4:00 p.m. matinee. Tony rushed out of school and down to the bank to withdraw some money for the movie and snacks. When he entered the bank, he encountered a long line of customers waiting for the bank tellers. A computer problem had closed all of the ATMs, so everyone had to do their banking in person.

By the time Tony got his cash, he was already late for the movie. As he dashed up to the theater, he saw his friends standing outside. Because attendance for the movie they wanted to see had recently fallen off, the theater was no longer showing that movie.

Then Wednesday Tony heard that his favorite music group would be performing locally, and tickets would go on sale this weekend. Promoters announced that due to the expected high demand for tickets, a $15 surcharge was being added to the price of each ticket. Tony thought the tickets were already expensive and didn't see why he should have to pay more when several other, less popular groups had played with no surcharge added.

Finally, today had been the most frustrating. Tony's parents owned a small landscaping business, and Tony always helped them find high school students to work during the summer. He had never had problems getting enough applicants for the available jobs. However, few people he talked with today were interested. They told him that since the unemployment rate was so low, many jobs were available that paid more and were not as hard work as landscaping. Now Tony thought back through his week's experiences and remembered Monday's economics discussion. "Maybe supply and demand affects my life more than I realize," he reflected.

IMPORTANCE OF MARKETING

In our private enterprise economy, it is not always easy to match production and consumption. Individual business people make decisions about what they will produce, and individual consumers make decisions about what they want to purchase. For the economy to work well, producers and consumers need information to help them make their decisions, so that producers will provide the types and amounts of products and services that consumers are willing and able to buy.

Marketing activities, when performed well, help to match production and consumption. As you learned in an earlier chapter, *marketing* is a set of activities that gets products from producers to consumers. From that very basic definition, you may think that marketing is simply transporting products. However, it is much more than that. It includes packaging, developing brand names, and determining prices. Marketing even involves financing and storing products until customers purchase them. Also, most products require some type of promotion. Marketing is involved in all of these activities and many more.

A more detailed definition will provide a better description of modern marketing. The American Marketing Association defines **marketing** as the process of planning and executing the conception, pricing, promotion, and distribution of ideas, goods, and services to create exchanges that satisfy individual and organizational objectives. Because marketing is the key tool in matching supply and demand, it can be viewed in another way as well. If marketing is successful, businesses will be able to sell their products and services and consumers will be able to obtain the things they want to purchase. Therefore, the goal of effective marketing is to create and maintain satisfying exchange relationships between buyers and sellers.

Every consumer comes into daily contact with marketing in one form or another. Whenever you see an advertisement on television or on the Internet, notice a truck being unloaded at a warehouse, or use a credit card to purchase a product, you are seeing marketing at work. Each retail store location, each form of advertising, each salesperson, and even each package in which a product is sold is a part of marketing. A great deal of business activity centers on marketing.

Millions of businesses worldwide engage in marketing as their primary business activities. Those organizations include **retailers**—businesses that sell directly to final consumers—and **wholesalers**—businesses that buy products from businesses and sell them to other businesses. The thousands of businesses that sell services, rather than products, are also included. In addition, advertising agencies provide promotional services, finance companies offer loans and other financial services, and transportation companies handle and move products. All of these types of business as well as many others that support the marketing efforts of other businesses are directly involved in marketing.

Many manufacturers have marketing departments with employees who do marketing tasks. For example, marketing department employees do market research, design products, and sell the products. Other types of marketing jobs involve advertising and sales promotion, customer service, credit, and insurance. The many jobs range from clerk to vice president in charge of all marketing activities. Well over one third of all people employed in the United States work in a marketing job or a marketing business.

■ NATURE OF MARKETING

When many people think of marketing, they think only of advertising and selling. However, many marketing activities must occur before a product can be advertised and sold. To better understand marketing, we will examine the major marketing activities, the cost of marketing activities, and the role of marketing in business.

FACTS AND FIGURES

It is estimated that the average consumer sees about 1 million marketing messages a year—about 3,000 a day. One trip to the supermarket alone can expose you to more than 10,000 marketing messages.

■ MARKETING ACTIVITIES

The most common marketing activities are listed below:

Buying — Obtaining product to be resold. This activity involves finding suppliers that can provide the right products in the right quality and quantity at a fair price.

Selling — Providing personalized and persuasive information to customers to help them buy the products and services they need.

Transporting — Moving products from where they were made to where consumers can buy them.

Storing — Holding products until customers need them, such as on shelves, in storage rooms, or in warehouses.

Financing — Providing money needed to pay for the various marketing activities, such as by obtaining credit when buying and extending credit when selling.

Researching — Studying buyer interests and needs, testing products, and gathering facts needed to make good marketing decisions.

Risk taking — Assuming the risk of losses that may occur from fire, theft, damage, or other circumstances.

Grading and valuing — Grouping goods according to size, quality, or other characteristics, and determining an appropriate price for products and services.

exam!
? 17

ILLUSTRATION 21-1

Storing is a common marketing activity. What are some others?

■ COST OF MARKETING

Whether the product is paper clips for offices or huge generators for utility companies, businesses must perform all eight marketing activities just described as the product moves from producer to customer. Because performing these activities requires many people and special equipment, the cost of marketing a product is sometimes higher than the cost of making that product. Therefore, perhaps half or more of the price you pay for a product may result from marketing expenses. Although this amount may appear high, the well-spent marketing dollar contributes much to the success of products and businesses as well as to the satisfaction of customers. Good marketing will make the product or service available to customers when and where they want it.

■ ROLE OF MARKETING

Marketing has not always been an important part of business. In the early 1900s, business conditions were much different than they are now. Customers had only a few products to choose from and a limited amount of money to spend. Usually only a few producers manufactured a product, and the manufacturing process was not very efficient. Demand for most products was greater than supply. As a result, most producers concentrated on making more kinds of products in greater quantities. Firms were **production oriented**; that is, decisions about what and how to produce received the most attention. Business people did not have to worry a great deal about marketing.

As production became more efficient and more businesses offered similar products, competition among businesses increased. Each business had to work hard to sell its products to customers when those customers saw they had many choices. Companies began to emphasize distribution to get their products to more customers. In addition, advertising and selling became important marketing tools as businesses tried to convince customers that their products were the best. Production was still considered the most important activity, but it was not enough for businesses to be successful. Businesses had become **sales oriented**; that is, they emphasized widespread distribution and promotion in order to sell the products produced.

However, with time, consumers realized that they had many choices of goods and services. Many businesses were competing with each other to sell the same product. Customers could demand products that met their needs, and a company would usually produce them. Companies began to realize it was not enough just to produce a variety of products; they had to produce the right products. Companies that produced what customers wanted and made buying easy for customers were more successful than those that did not.

Today, more and more businesses are focusing on customer needs. They have become **customer oriented**; that is, they direct the activities of the company toward satisfying customers. Keeping the needs

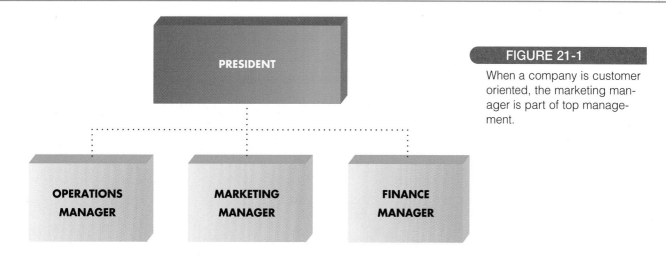

FIGURE 21-1

When a company is customer oriented, the marketing manager is part of top management.

of the consumer uppermost in mind during the design, production, and distribution of a product is called the **marketing concept.** —Exam! ?.5

A company that has adopted the marketing concept will have a marketing manager who is part of top management and is involved in all major decisions, as illustrated in Figure 21-1. Marketing personnel will work closely with the other people in the business to make sure that the company keeps the needs of customers in mind in all operations. The company's success will be determined by more than current profits. While profit is important, long-term success depends on satisfying customers so that they will continue to buy from the company.

■ MARKET DETERMINATION

Before a company decides to make and distribute a product, it must determine the market it wants to serve. Here, **market** refers to the types of buyers a business wishes to attract and where those buyers are located. All companies need to clearly identify their markets.

WHOM TO SERVE A company has many potential customers for every product. Some people may be searching for the product, while others do not currently want the product and will have to be convinced to buy it. Some people will be very easy to reach, while others are quite difficult to contact. For cost reasons, it is usually unwise to try to reach all potential customers. Therefore, a business identifies several groups of potential customers and then decides which group or groups will be the best markets for its product.

Marketers often develop a customer profile based on population characteristics, such as age, gender, family status, education, income, and occupation, to group consumers. A clothing manufacturer, for example, could handle women's or men's clothing, clothing for children or adults, casual clothing or the latest fashions, and so on. The producer of cellular telephones may want to attract families, people concerned about their safety, or business people. Businesses can decide to

ILLUSTRATION 21-2

How can a business identify potential customers for its product or service?

serve one or more markets. Companies choose a market based on the opportunities for success that the market presents. For example, an attractive market may have few existing competitors, a large number of customers with a need for the product, and customers with sufficient money to spend on such a product. If the business has the ability to produce a product that will satisfy the needs of that market, then it is a good market for the business to serve.

WHERE TO SERVE Producers often limit the scope of their business operations to certain geographic areas. Marketing managers study sections of a city, state, country, or continent to determine whether their product might sell more successfully in one area than another. Climate, for example, may cause a small producer of air conditioners to concentrate its marketing efforts on countries with hot and humid climates for its markets, whereas the maker of snow skis may concentrate on areas where there is an abundance of cold weather and mountains. Some products may sell better on the coasts than in the middle of the country, or in rural areas better than cities. Finding the best marketing locations enables a business to achieve the most sales for its marketing dollar.

IDENTIFYING TARGET MARKETS Companies can produce goods and services that meet consumers' needs better if they know who their customers are, where they are located, and what they want and need. Many companies spend a great deal of money on market research before they begin to develop products. **Market research** is the study of a company's current and prospective customers.

Companies use market research to identify their target markets. **Target markets** are groups of customers with very similar needs to whom the company plans to sell its product. If the company can find a group of people with very similar needs, it can more easily produce a product that will satisfy everyone in the group. On the other hand, if people in the group have needs that are quite different, it will be almost impossible to develop a product that will satisfy each of them.

Imagine developing a product like a bicycle. It can be made in a variety of sizes and shapes with a number of special features. No one bicycle will satisfy everyone's needs. Long-distance racers want something very different from what the weekend rider desires. However, if you could find a group of people with very similar needs, you could successfully design a bicycle for that group. If you identified the groups depicted in Figure 21-2, each with unique needs for your product, your bicycle company could choose to design a slightly different product for each group.

■ ELEMENTS OF MARKETING

Marketing managers have many decisions to make. These decisions center on four elements of marketing: (1) the *product,* (2) its *price,* (3) *distribution* (sometimes referred to as *place*), and (4) *promotion.* Planning each element involves answering some important questions. For example, assume that you want to market a new product. You must answer the following questions related to the four elements of

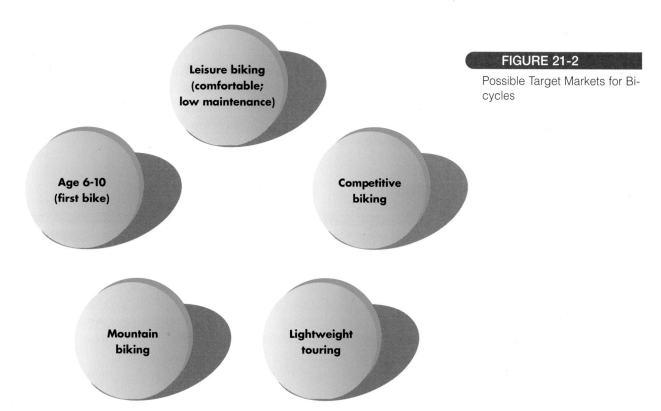

FIGURE 21-2

Possible Target Markets for Bicycles

Leisure biking
(comfortable;
low maintenance)

Age 6-10
(first bike)

Competitive
biking

Mountain
biking

Lightweight
touring

CYBER COMMUNICATION

The world of e-mail has its own language. Regular users will quickly pick up its distinctive vocabulary.

- *Spamming* refers to sending mass, unsolicited messages or advertising (called *spam*).
- *Flaming* is the act of sending angry or insulting messages (called *flames*).
- *Emoticons* are icons, built by combining various letters or symbols, used to reflect emotion. Because they can be created with any keyboard, they are popular in e-mail messages to communicate meanings (such as sarcasm, surprise, confusion, sadness, or happiness).
- *Abbreviations* are frequently used in order to speed up keying. *BTW* means "by the way." *IMHO* means "in my humble opinion."

ACTIVITY Under what circumstances is it appropriate to use e-mail vocabulary and "tools," such as emoticons? Are there instances when it would not be suitable? Write a one-page article describing both kinds of occasions. If you have e-mail access, include any personal experiences you have had.

marketing: (1) Will you make the product in one size and color, or in several? (2) Will you price the product high, medium, or low? (3) Will you sell the product in retail stores or over the Internet? (4) Will you use newspaper, radio, television, or Internet advertising?

The blend of all decisions related to the four elements of marketing—product, price, distribution, and promotion—is called the **marketing mix**. The marketing mix for a new product may be to design the item for young adults, give it a low price, sell it through retail stores, and advertise it on the radio. Or it could be to produce a medium-priced item to be advertised on television and sold door-to-door to senior citizens. Can you identify the marketing mix for one of the businesses that Tony Taylor thought about in the chapter-opening scenario?

Several companies marketing the same product may use very different marketing mixes, because they made different decisions. Furthermore, they must review their decisions frequently, because conditions change constantly. Changes in general economic conditions, changes in consumer needs, and the development of new or improved products by competitors are factors that may require a change in the marketing mix. Next, you will learn about the decisions involved in each marketing mix element.

■ PRODUCT

The first marketing mix element is the product. **Product** can be defined as all attributes, both tangible and intangible, that customers receive in exchange for the purchase price. For example, when consumers buy a computer, they are also buying the company's customer service and technical support as well as other intangibles, such as the prestige of the brand name. All of these attributes are part of the product. Products include services as well as physical goods. A critical question relating to the product is: What do customers want? Product planning and development deal with finding answers to that question.

By identifying the target market for a product and knowing what customers in that market want, the company can design a product to fit those customers. Market information can help marketers develop a product strategy that includes decisions such as:

1. The *number* of items to produce.
2. The *physical features* the product should possess, such as the size, shape, color, and weight.
3. The *quality* preferred by the target market.
4. The *number of different models* and the *required features* of each model needed to serve the various markets the company wants to attract.
5. The *packaging features* of the item, such as the color and the shape of the package, as well as the information printed on the package.
6. The *brand name* to use.
7. Product *guarantees* and *services* the customers would like.
8. The *image* to be communicated to customers by the products, features, packaging, and brand name.

■ PRICE

The second mix element around which marketing decisions are made is price. **Price** is the amount of money given to acquire a product. The many decisions a company makes during product development influence the price. First, the price must be high enough to cover the costs of producing and marketing the product. If the company decided to manufacture a high-quality product, it would likely have to set a higher price to cover its costs than it would for a low-quality product. The number of competing products and their prices, the demand for the product, and whether the product will be sold for cash or credit are some of the many factors that influence price decisions.

When making price decisions, a company must do more than just set a price that customers will pay for the product. It must decide what price to charge other companies that buy and resell the product. Will the company offer coupons, discounts, or other promotional methods to attract customers? Will it allow customers to bargain for a lower price or trade in a used product for a new one? As you can see, pricing is not an easy marketing decision.

■ DISTRIBUTION

The third element around which marketing decisions are made is distribution. Distribution decisions relate to the economic concept of *place utility,* which you studied in Chapter 3. *Place utility* means that the product must be in a place where customers need or want it. **Distribution (or place),** therefore, is the set of activities required to transport and store products, and make them available to customers.

Marketing managers must select businesses to handle products as they move from the producer to the consumer. Many manufacturers prefer to

— Exam 1
? 20

use other businesses to sell their products rather than try to reach consumers directly. Therefore, they may sell their products to retailers or to wholesalers, which then sell to retailers. Choosing the various routes that products will follow as they are distributed and the businesses that will sell them to consumers are important marketing decisions.

Planning distribution also includes the actual physical handling of the products and the customer service provided in processing orders. Have you ever opened a product you purchased, only to find it damaged or missing pieces? Have you ordered something from a catalog or the Internet and have the order lost, filled with the wrong merchandise, or sent to an incorrect address? Each of these examples describes a problem with a company's distribution system and will result in dissatisfied customers as well as a loss of sales and profits for the company.

■ PROMOTION

The fourth marketing mix element for which decisions must be made is promotion. **Promotion** means providing information to consumers that will assist them in making a decision and persuade them to purchase a product or service. The major methods of promotion are advertising and personal selling. You will learn about other types of promotion in a later chapter.

Promotional decisions for a digital camera might involve selecting advertising as the main method to use and deciding whether to advertise in magazines or by mail directly to prospective customers. Marketing managers decide when to advertise and how frequently to show the ad. Then they must decide whether to use sales demonstrations in stores or to have product demonstrations at consumer electronics shows. Managers must also decide the type of information to communicate to consumers and whether to try to communicate directly with each customer or use more impersonal messages that can reach a larger audience at a time.

The type of product and its price influence promotional decisions. The strategy for promoting an expensive piece of jewelry will be much different from that for promoting tennis shoes.

While the product and its price provide general guides for promotion, marketing managers must consider many other factors before developing the actual promotions. For example, the company will budget only a certain amount of money for promotion. Managers must decide when to spend the money and how much to spend for advertising, displays, and other types of promotion. They must consider what promotions competitors are using and what information consumers need in order to decide to buy.

■ MARKETING PLAN

All the marketing decisions for a particular product must work together for the product to succeed. For example, advertising may be timed to

FACTS AND FIGURES

Eastman Kodak wanted to attract young consumers to its one-time-use cameras. Kodak developed a "Through Your Eyes" promotion by sponsoring a new teen rock band, Youngstown. The band played concerts at various U.S. malls, where souvenir pictures were snapped of the band members with their fans. In addition, "Through Your Eyes" retail packages were sold, featuring the band's CD and a Kodak one-time-use camera.

coincide with a product's introduction. To help coordinate marketing activities, businesses develop a marketing plan. The **marketing plan** is a detailed written description of all marketing activities that a business must accomplish in order to sell its products. It describes the goals the business wants to accomplish, the target markets it wants to serve, the marketing mixes it will use for each product, and the tactics that make up the marketing strategy. It identifies the ways in which the business will evaluate its marketing to determine if the activities were successful and the goals were accomplished. The marketing plan is written for a specific time period (often one year).

The top marketing executive develops the marketing plan, based on information from many other people. Market research will be very important in developing a marketing plan. Once a written plan is completed, all of the people involved in marketing activities can use it to guide their decisions about each marketing mix element and to coordinate their efforts as they complete the planned activities.

■ THE PRODUCT LIFE CYCLE

Successful products move through rather predictable stages throughout their product lives. They are introduced, and then their sales and profits increase rapidly until a point at which they level off. Eventually, both profits and sales will decline, as newer products replace the old one. The **product life cycle** is the four stages of sales and profit performance through which all brands of a product progress: introduction, growth, maturity, and decline. Figure 21-3 is a graphical depiction of sales and profits at different stages of the product life cycle.

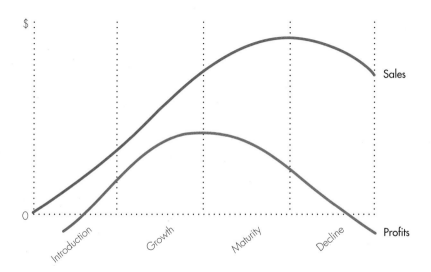

FIGURE 21-3

Sales and profits follow a predictable pattern as products progress through each stage of the product life cycle.

■ INTRODUCTION

In the **introduction stage,** a brand-new product enters the market. Initially, there is only one brand of the product available for consumers to purchase. The new product is quite different from, and hopefully better than, products customers are currently using. While every product has gone through the introduction stage at some time, examples of products that were recently in that stage include Web-ready cellular telephones, high definition television (HDTV), and portable audio players that can download digital music files from the Internet.

When a company introduces a product, it is concerned about successfully producing and distributing. The company needs to inform prospective customers about the brand-new product and its uses, since people will be unfamiliar with it. There is no competition from the same type of product, but customers will probably be using other older products. The company must show customers how the new product is better than the products they are currently using. Initially, only a few customers will buy the product, but their experience will often determine whether other people will want to buy it as well.

The costs of producing and marketing a new product are usually very high, resulting in a loss or very low profits for the firm initially. The company is counting on future sales to make a profit. If a product is successfully introduced, an increasing number of consumers will accept the new product, sales will start to grow rapidly, and profits will emerge.

■ GROWTH

When competitors see the success of the new product, they will want to get into that market as well. When several brands of the new product are available, the market moves into the **growth stage** of the life cycle. If customers like the new product, they will begin buying it regularly and telling others about it, so more and more customers are now regular purchasers.

In the growth stage, each company tries to attract customers to its specific brand. Companies attempt to improve their brands by adding features that they hope will satisfy customers. They also add to their distribution to make the product more readily available to the growing market. Most companies make a profit in this stage. Profits are likely to increase as companies sell enough of the product to cover the research and development costs. Examples of products that have been in the growth stage recently are digital video cameras, personal digital assistants (PDAs), and sports utility vehicles (SUVs).

■ MATURITY

A product in the maturity stage has been purchased by large numbers of customers and has become quite profitable. In the **maturity stage,** the product has many competing brands with very similar features. Customers have a hard time identifying differences among the brands but may have developed a loyalty to one or a very few brands.

In this stage, companies emphasize the promotion of their brand name, packaging, a specific image, and often the price of the product. Because there are so many customers, each business has to distribute the product widely, adding to their costs. Competition becomes intense. Companies must spend a lot on promotion and reduce prices, because customers have many brands from which to choose. Profits usually fall even though sales may still increase. Products in the maturity stage include automobiles, desktop computers, personal care products such as toothpaste and deodorant, and many other products that you use regularly and purchase without a great deal of thought.

ILLUSTRATION 21-3

How might a fast-food company respond to the maturity stage of the product life cycle?

One way that businesses respond to the maturity stage of the life cycle is to look for new markets. Businesses often begin to move into international markets as competition increases in their home countries. As fast-food companies found fewer and fewer attractive locations for new stores in the U.S., they began to open outlets in Canada, Europe, and Mexico. Now they are expanding into South America and even Russia and China.

■ DECLINE

Many products stay in the maturity stage of the life cycle for a long time. However, sooner or later products move into a decline stage. The **decline stage** occurs when a new product is introduced that is much better or easier to use, and customers begin to switch from the old product to the new product. As more and more customers are attracted to the new product, the companies selling the old product will soon see declines in profits and sales. The companies may not be able to improve the older products enough to compete with the new products, so they drop them from the market when declining profits no longer support their existence.

Some companies have been able to move old products out of the decline stage by finding new uses for them. For example, baby oil is now being used as a suntan product, and baking soda is used to remove odors from refrigerators and cat litter boxes. If companies cannot save a product from the decline stage, they will attempt to sell their remaining inventory to the customers who still prefer it. However, they will spend as little money as possible while marketing the product and will not produce any more.

■ TYPES OF CONSUMER PRODUCTS

When making marketing decisions, marketers need to understand how customers shop for and use products. Products can be classified as either industrial goods or consumer goods. **Industrial goods** are products designed for use by another business. Frequently, industrial goods are purchased in large quantities, are made to special order for a specific customer, or are sold to a selected group of buyers located within a limited geographic area. Examples of industrial goods include bricks purchased by a building contractor, aluminum purchased by an aircraft manufacturer, and computers and computer supplies purchased by accounting firms. Many, but not all, industrial goods are used to produce other products or are incorporated into the products being produced. Some are used in the operation of the business.

Consumer goods are products designed for personal or home use. Jewelry, furniture, magazines, soft drinks, and computer games are some of the many products used by consumers. Consumer goods require careful marketing attention, because there are so many products and brands available and so many possible customers located throughout the world.

Depending on who is making the purchase and how they will use it, however, a product may be both a consumer good and an industrial good. Gasoline and laptop computers, for instance, may be purchased by consumers in small quantities or by businesses in large quantities.

To look at the attributes of consumer goods more specifically, marketers group them into four categories: convenience goods, shopping goods, specialty goods, and unsought goods. The categories are based on (1) how important the product is to the customer and (2) whether the customer is willing to spend time to compare products and brands before making a decision to buy. Companies make different marketing decisions, depending on which category of consumer goods they are selling.

■ CONVENIENCE GOODS

Convenience goods are inexpensive items that consumers purchase regularly without a great deal of thought. Consumers are not willing to shop around for these products because they purchase them often, the many competing products do not differ much from each other, and they don't cost much money. Therefore, marketers will need to sell their convenience goods through many retail outlets that are conveniently located close to where people work and live. Products that are usually treated as convenience goods are candy, milk, soft drinks, pencils, soap, and many other inexpensive household items.

■ SHOPPING GOODS

Products that consumers purchase less frequently than convenience goods, usually have a higher price, and require some buying thought are called **shopping goods**. Customers see important differences between brands of these products in terms of price and features. Therefore, they are willing to shop at several businesses and compare products and brands before they make a purchase. Shopping goods do not have to be sold in as many places as convenience goods. They need effective promotion so customers can make informed decisions. Cars, furniture, large appliances, and houses are all examples of shopping goods for most people.

■ SPECIALTY GOODS

Specialty goods are products that customers insist upon having and are willing to search for until they find them. Customers who decide that only one product or brand will satisfy them will shop until they locate and buy that brand. Marketers place their specialty goods in fewer businesses within a shopping area, price them higher than competing

ILLUSTRATION 21-4

How are specialty goods different from other types of goods?

products and brands, and need not promote them as much as other types of consumer products. Examples of specialty goods are designer clothing, expensive jewelry, and certain brands of cameras, computers, or automobiles.

■ UNSOUGHT GOODS

Customers do not shop for some products because they do not have a strong need for them. Such products are known as **unsought goods**, and they present a difficult marketing problem. Life insurance, encyclopedias, and funeral services are unsought by most consumers. A company marketing unsought goods will usually have to go to the customer and use personal selling to discuss the need for the product. Unless the customer recognizes a need that the product can satisfy, the product will remain unsold.

■ SUCCESSFUL MARKETING STRATEGIES

Marketing managers cannot afford to guess about the types of marketing mixes to use. Marketing is too expensive and customers have too many choices for businesses to risk making mistakes. Marketers use concepts such as the product life cycle and consumer goods categories to plan effective marketing mixes. For example, if a product is in the growth stage, the mix will be quite different than if it is in the maturity stage. If consumers view a product as a specialty good, marketers will emphasize different mix elements than if it is a convenience good. Marketers study markets and competition and use their knowledge of marketing to make decisions that will satisfy customer needs and result in a profit for the company.

Many consumer complaints today involve marketing activities. Misleading advertisements, poor customer service, high prices, and poor delivery are all marketing problems. Businesses must be as careful in making marketing decisions as they need to be in producing a quality product. In the next two chapters, we will examine each part of the marketing mix in more detail. You will learn how businesses plan products and use marketing activities to satisfy customers and attract them away from competing businesses.

FACTS AND FIGURES

Marketing to children continues to be a controversial issue. The Federal Trade Commission's Children's Online Privacy Protection Act requires children's Web site publishers to post comprehensive privacy policies on their sites. In addition, the sites must notify parents about their information practices and obtain parental consent before collecting any personal information from children under age 13.

MANAGEMENT CLOSE-UP

RETAILERS THAT CHANGED BUSINESS

Most manufacturers of consumer goods rely on retailers to provide the connection with the customers who will purchase their products. The retailers purchase the products from the manufacturer, stock them in stores that are close to the locations where customers live, advertise and sell the products, and often offer delivery of the products and many customer services. Retailers provide these important marketing functions for manufacturers.

A few retailers have changed the way business is done. Because of their ideas, they forced their competitors to respond or risk going out of business.

One of the first was Sears Roebuck. In the late 1800s and early 1900s, some of the largest retailers reached their customers by mail. They sent catalogs to people all over the country and filled the customer orders by mail or by trucks and trains. Sears decided customers wanted faster service and the opportunity to examine merchandise before making a purchase. The company began building large stores filled with a large variety of products. Customers flocked to the stores, and Sears became the largest retailer in the world.

While Sears stores were located in large and mid-sized cities, Sam Walton saw opportunities in the thousands of small communities around the country. Wal-Mart grew because of its emphasis on carefully chosen locations, working with manufacturers to buy at the lowest prices, developing an efficient product distribution system, and creating a friendly shopping experience. Because of those efforts, Wal-Mart could offer lower prices than most other retailers. With this new philosophy of retailing, Wal-Mart replaced Sears as the world's largest retailer.

Today, a new form of retailing is developing, led by Jeff Bezos. Mr. Bezos recognized the new Internet consumers. By developing an easy-to-use Web site and offering customers secure online purchases, rapid product delivery, and effective customer service, Amazon.com developed into the largest e-tailer, with revenues approaching one billion dollars.

In each example, the success of the companies resulted from finding new ways to offer products and services to consumers. By performing marketing activities better than their competitors, each company has become a leading retailer.

THINK CRITICALLY

1. Why were major retailers using catalogs and mail order in the late 1800s and early 1900s to sell products to their customers? What changes were occurring in the U.S. that provided the opportunity for Sears Roebuck to change the way products were sold?
2. Review the eight marketing activities described in the chapter and suggest which of the activities were most important to the success of Wal-Mart. Why were many of Wal-Mart's competitors not able to offer the same low prices to customers?
3. Do you believe that an e-tailer like Amazon.com will ever replace Wal-Mart as the world's largest retailer? Why or why not?

CHAPTER CONCEPTS

- Marketing helps to balance the supply of products produced with the demand for those products. The goal of effective marketing is to create and maintain satisfying exchanges between buyers and sellers.
- Every business is involved in marketing. Marketing is the primary activity for retailers and wholesalers. More than one third of all people employed in the U.S. complete marketing activities or work for a marketing business.
- Marketing is more than advertising and selling. It involves eight activities: buying, selling, transporting, storing, financing, researching, risk taking, and grading and valuing.
- During the 1900s, marketing approaches evolved from production-oriented to sales-oriented and finally to customer-oriented. Companies that operate according to the marketing concept keep the needs of consumers uppermost in mind during the design, production, and distribution of a product.
- Businesses must decide whom to serve and where to serve when planning marketing. They use marketing research to identify target markets—customers with very similar needs that the business wants to serve.
- Marketing managers make decisions about the four elements of marketing: the product, its price, distribution, and promotion. Together, these decisions form the marketing mix.
- Companies prepare a written marketing plan to coordinate the many decisions and activities involved in marketing. The top marketing executive usually prepares the marketing plan with information gathered from many other people.
- The product life cycle consists of four stages of sales and profit performance that products move through during their time on the market. The stages are introduction, growth, maturity, and decline.
- Products are classified as either industrial or consumer goods, based on who purchases them and how they will use the products. Consumer goods can be classified into four categories based on their importance to consumers and how much time consumers are willing to spend making the buying decisions. The categories are convenience, shopping, specialty, and unsought goods.

BUILD VOCABULARY POWER

Define the following terms and concepts.

1. marketing
2. retailers
3. wholesalers
4. buying
5. selling
6. transporting
7. storing
8. financing

9. researching
10. risk taking
11. grading and valuing
12. production oriented
13. sales oriented
14. customer oriented
15. marketing concept
16. market
17. market research
18. target markets
19. marketing mix
20. product
21. price
22. distribution (place)
23. promotion
24. marketing plan
25. product life cycle
26. introduction stage
27. growth stage
28. maturity stage
29. decline stage
30. industrial goods
31. consumer goods
32. convenience goods
33. shopping goods
34. specialty goods
35. unsought goods

REVIEW FACTS

1. In our economy, who makes decisions about what will be produced and what will be purchased?
2. What is the goal of effective marketing?
3. What is the difference between a retailer and a wholesaler?
4. What percentage of all U.S. employees work in a marketing job or for a marketing business?
5. How do customers benefit, even if more than half of the price of the products they purchase goes to pay for marketing activities?
6. Why did businesses change from a production orientation to a customer orientation during the last century?
7. What two questions must a firm answer about its customers when identifying a market to serve?
8. How does a target market make it easier for a company to produce a product that will satisfy customer needs?
9. What are the four elements of the marketing mix?
10. When marketing managers make decisions about distribution, what economic concept are they applying?
11. Why are the physical handling of the product and customer service important parts of distribution planning?
12. What are the two major methods of promotion?
13. How does the amount of competition change as products progress through the stages of the product life cycle?
14. How can the same product be both an industrial good and a consumer good?
15. What are the two factors that determine the categories of consumer goods?

DISCUSS IDEAS

1. In what ways are trucking companies, banks, and warehouses marketing businesses?

2. Explain how valuing and grading are used in the marketing of products you would purchase at a supermarket.
3. Why is it important for a business to conduct market research to determine the markets to be served before deciding what to produce and sell?
4. Identify several products for which you believe the cost of marketing would be well below half of the price customers would pay. Then identify several others for which you believe the cost of marketing would be well over half of the final price. What differences influence the cost of marketing for these products?
5. Do you believe that use of the Internet by businesses will increase or decrease the amount of marketing they must do? Do you believe it will increase or decrease the cost of marketing for those companies? Why?
6. What are some examples of goods or services that would sell well only in specific geographic locations?
7. How might customers know if a company has a customer orientation rather than a sales orientation?
8. How can a product's package be used to satisfy customers?
9. How do the other three elements of the marketing mix influence the price of a product? What could a marketing manager do with other mix elements to increase or decrease a product's price?
10. Why is a consumer willing to spend time shopping for some products but not for others?

ANALYZE INFORMATION

1. Select any product that you use regularly. Using the eight marketing activities listed in the chapter, give an example showing how each activity was completed between the time the company produced the product and the time someone purchased it.

2. Use magazines, newspapers, or the Internet to find examples that illustrate each of the four elements of the marketing mix—product, price, distribution, and promotion. Either by cutting and pasting the examples or by drawing the examples on posterboard (your teacher will give you specific instructions), create a collage illustrating the concept of a marketing mix.
3. On a separate sheet of paper, complete the following table for the four products listed by determining the total cost of the product and the percentage of the final product price that was spent on marketing.

	Product 1	Product 2	Product 3	Product 4
Raw Materials	$6.20	$28.00	$12,650.00	$ .78
Other Product Costs	3.80	56.50	2,500.00	.14

(continued)

	Product 1	Product 2	Product 3	Product 4
Operating Expenses	4.30	74.00	4,825.00	.32
Marketing Expenses	14.90	96.50	3,500.00	2.50
Total Cost	___	___	___	___
Retail Price	45.20	576.00	32,750.00	4.80
Marketing as a % of Retail Price	___	___	___	___

4. Participate in a debate with other class members. Your teacher will assign you to one side of the issue or the other and will give you specific instructions for the debate. The issue is: Marketing causes people to spend money for things they otherwise would not buy and do not need. Do you agree or disagree?

5. Interview 10 people to determine how they purchase jeans. Ask each of them the following questions:

a. Where do you usually buy your jeans?

b. What product features are important to you when you are deciding to buy?

c. How important is price in your decision to purchase your jeans?

d. Do you usually buy one brand?

e. Do you usually look in several stores before you buy a pair of jeans?

Based on each person's answers, determine whether he or she is treating jeans as a convenience, shopping, specialty, or unsought good. Write a short report discussing your findings and your conclusions. Include a chart or graph illustrating your findings.

SOLVE BUSINESS PROBLEMS

CASE 21-1

The personal computer market is becoming very competitive, and it is getting more and more difficult for computer manufacturers to make a profit. Technology changes rapidly, so if a company has not sold its inventory of one model of computer when a competitor introduces a newer, faster, more powerful model, it often has to sell its older model at a loss. Many computer purchasers are not brand-loyal and either look for a lower price or expect the manufacturer to include related products, such as a monitor, printer, scanner, or large amount of software with the new computer.

One computer manufacturer began a new marketing program that offered customers a free computer. The free computer was not the manufacturer's latest model. The offer also did not include a large monitor or additional equipment or software. Instead, the manufacturer required the customer to sign a contract to use the manufacturer's Internet service for at least three years at a cost of $25.95 a month. Typically, consumers could buy the same service for as little as $14.95 a month from other companies.

Think Critically:

1. Which stage of the product life cycle do you believe computers are in, based on the case information? Why?
2. In which consumer product category do you believe consumers classify computers, based on the case information? Why?
3. Describe the target market that you believe might be attracted to the manufacturer's offer of a free computer.
4. What are the advantages and disadvantages of offering consumers a computer that is not the company's latest model?

CASE 21-2

The Willomette Company manufactures small household appliances, such as toasters, blenders, and food processors. Ron Willomette started the company 20 years ago as a sole proprietorship. Initially, Mr. Willomette reconditioned and resold used appliances that other companies had manufactured. Now he has incorporated the business and has two manufacturing plants that produce his own brand of appliances. The Willomette Company has a full line of over 50 models of products that are sold throughout the United States.

In the past five years, competition from foreign companies in the small appliance market has increased. While the competition hasn't hurt Willomette yet, company executives don't want to wait until sales and profits start to decline before acting. One vice president recommended that Willomette begin a program of international marketing. Based on the traveling she has done, she believes that the demand for Willomette's appliances would be very strong in Europe and several countries in Africa and South America. Because there has been strong customer acceptance of the company's products in the U.S., she believes Willomette should have no trouble selling the same products in other countries.

Think Critically:

1. Which of the major marketing activities would Willomette have to perform to sell its products in international markets?
2. How does the marketing concept relate to the decision Willomette must make about entering international markets?
3. Do you agree that products that are successful in the U.S. will also be successful in other countries? Explain.
4. What would Willomette have to do if it wanted to try to increase the demand for its products in the U.S. by selling industrial products?

PROJECT: MY BUSINESS, INC.

To market your products effectively, you will need to identify the target market for your business. Then you must determine how customers will view your product as they make decisions to buy. The activities in this section of the project will help you understand your customers, so you can develop an effective marketing mix.

DATA COLLECTION

1. Locate books, newspaper and magazine articles, Web resources, and other information sources that describe people who are interested in healthy lifestyles and nutrition. Make a list of the sources of information that will help you describe possible target markets for your juice bar and provide brief descriptions of the information in each of the sources you list.
2. Review advertisements from other businesses that might compete with your juice bar. For each business, prepare a description of the target market it appears they are appealing to and the key part of their marketing mix that they are advertising.

3. Using library or Internet resources, locate several marketing-oriented magazines or trade journals that you could consult for information. Also, identify some marketing-related professional organizations or trade associations that might be helpful to you.

ANALYSIS

1. Using the categories of consumer goods listed in the chapter, determine if customers will treat your product as a convenience, shopping, specialty, or unsought good. Describe how that decision will influence the way you market your products.
2. Markets are made up of many segments of people who have one or more similar characteristics. Segments of a market can be identified that have one or more strong needs or wants in common. What market segment(s) can you identify for your product?
3. Develop a detailed customer profile of one or more target markets that you can serve successfully. Make sure that your profile description includes both an identification of the target market and their important needs related to your product. For the principal target market, prepare a general description of the marketing mix you believe you should provide to satisfy those consumers. Prepare a marketing plan that describes the goals your business should accomplish, the target market you want to serve, the marketing mix you will use, and the tactics that make up your marketing strategy.

PRODUCT DEVELOPMENT AND DISTRIBUTION

OBJECTIVES

22-1 Identify why product development decisions are important to consumers as well as businesses.

22-2 Describe the three levels of product development and the types of product selection.

22-3 Discuss how packaging and branding improve product sales and customer satisfaction.

22-4 Discuss the important factors to be considered when selecting channels of distribution.

22-5 Describe the characteristics of major forms of transportation used to distribute products.

22-6 Give examples of product-handling procedures that improve product distribution.

DECISIONS, DECISIONS

lexis Converse sat at her computer in the purchasing office late into the night. She was challenged by a crisis facing her company. A major piece of manufacturing equipment had failed today and could not be repaired. Each day that the equipment was not operational would cost the company several thousand dollars in lost production and sales.

The machine was over 10 years old, and it had worked well for most of the time the company owned it. In discussing its replacement with the production manager, Alexis agreed that they should replace the machine with the same brand. However, there were now two new models to consider. Alexis could purchase the equipment directly from the manufacturer from its location in Italy or from an equipment distributor located two states away. The manufacturer would take eight days to deliver, whereas the

distributor could have one model available in two days and the other in four.

Alexis was concerned about installation and maintenance. She wanted to make sure the new machine would not break down again. The manufacturer had a specialist who would travel to the plant to install and make sure the equipment was working. That company also included a five-year warranty with onsite service, but it added 25 percent to the cost of the equipment. Alexis had heard that the distributor could help with the installation but did not provide an additional warranty or service. Delays or problems in installation would only add to the company's losses.

All Alexis wanted to do was to get the equipment replaced and the company back into production. Why did these decisions have to be so difficult?

You learned in Chapter 21 that companies develop a marketing mix to satisfy customers and make a profit. The marketing mix is made up of the product, distribution, price, and promotion plans. Offering products that meet the needs of customers would seem to be a company's most important responsibility. The product is important but must be carefully coordinated with each of the other mix elements. In this chapter, we will examine how companies plan products and make distribution decisions.

■ PRODUCT DEVELOPMENT

As you learned in Chapter 21, a *product* consists of all attributes, both tangible and intangible, that customers receive in exchange for the purchase price. It includes both physical goods and services. Some products are very simple and easy for the customer to understand and use, while others are very complex. Because of the variety of customer needs, the uses for products, and the number of competing companies producing and selling products, product development decisions must be made carefully. If companies produce the wrong products in the wrong quantities without the features and services customers need, they will have invested a great deal of time and money with no chance to sell

ILLUSTRATION 22-1

Why should a company make product development decisions very carefully?

the products at a profit. They will quickly lose out to competitors who make better product decisions.

Business people and consumers usually hold very different perceptions of a product. Business people think of their products as what they have to offer to customers. On the other hand, consumers are more likely to think of products as ways to satisfy their needs. The company that manufactures the machine Alexis needed to purchase at the beginning of the chapter designed a product to perform a specific production function. The company is expert in the technology of equipment design, so it builds what it believes to be a good product that customers will prefer, compared to alternatives. Alexis wants a good piece of equipment but is also very concerned about delivery, installation services, maintenance, and cost. If the equipment manufacturer does not carefully consider all of Alexis's needs, it probably won't make the sale.

Even the simplest products are made up of several components. An inexpensive handheld calculator consists of the operating unit to make the calculations, a case, display, and keys. It may be battery operated or use solar power or electricity. It could have a backlight to illuminate the display in the dark. It could be pocket- or desk-sized, and on and on. Also, it might come in a variety of colors and include special mathematical functions, a protective case, and an instruction manual. Given the combination of features, the price of the calculator could range from a very few dollars to as much as $50 or more. If you were the person responsible for designing a calculator to sell, what combination of design features would you include? This example shows that product planning can be very complex. Businesses have many choices in designing products. In developing their product strategy, marketers pay close attention to their customers' needs and wishes.

■ PRODUCT DESIGN LEVELS

There are three levels of product design—a basic product, an enhanced product, and an extended product. The **basic product** is the physical product in its simplest form. It should be easy for consumers to understand and see how it can meet a need. The basic product of one company will usually be similar to that of its competitors.

The basic product will meet an important consumer need. However, most consumers are attempting to satisfy several needs at one time with a purchase or have very specific needs different from other consumers. In that case, the basic product will not be satisfactory. Therefore, a business will develop an enhanced product. **An enhanced product** is a product that offers different features and options for the consumer. For example, a basic computer can be produced in desktop or notebook form. It can have different screen and hard drive sizes, offer DVD, an advanced speaker system, and many other features. If you have looked at the Web site of an online computer manufacturer, you can see the many options available to prospective purchasers. Choices are grouped by categories of customers, such as business, home office, education, and family, making it easier for customers to design the computer system they need.

The third level of product development is to plan extended products. **An extended product** is a product that includes additional features that are not part of the physical product but increase its usability. Examples are customer service, information on effective use of the products, and even additional products that improve the use of the original purchase. If you purchase a new digital video camera, you will need tapes to begin filming. In addition, a tripod may be helpful to make sure the video images are not shaky. Editing software, instructional videotapes, and even lens filters to create special effects may be useful to some but not all customers. The right combination of choices allows customers to get just the right product to meet very specialized needs.

Companies may offer a *warranty* (a statement from the seller about the product's qualities or performance) or a *guarantee* (an assurance from the seller that a product will perform to your satisfaction for a certain period of time). This can help reassure the customer about the product.

■ PRODUCT SELECTION

After designing the product, companies must make another set of decisions to plan the product mix element. The first choice is to decide whether to offer a product line. A **product line** is a group of similar products with obvious variations in the design and quality to meet the needs of distinct customer groups. New and small companies may

CAREER CONNECTION

MARKETING MANAGER

The objective of any business is to market its products or services profitably. Marketing managers develop the business's detailed marketing strategy. They determine the demand for products and services; identify potential consumers; develop a pricing strategy; monitor trends in new products and services; and oversee product development and promotion.

For marketing management positions, some employers prefer a college or even a graduate degree in business administration, with an emphasis on marketing. Courses in business law, economics, accounting, finance, mathematics, and statistics are also desirable.

Persons interested in a marketing management career should be creative, motivated, flexible, decisive, and able to handle stress. The ability to communicate persuasively, both orally and in writing, is crucial.

For more career information about marketing managers, check your library or the Internet for resources.

begin by offering only one category of product to its customers. That product may have choices of features, options, and enhancements, but the basic product is the same for all customers. With more experience and resources, the company may decide to expand its product line.

One of the obvious ways to expand a product line is to offer different sizes of the product. That can be done with the serving sizes of food items as well as with the sizes of automobiles. As an example, automobile manufacturers have had a great deal of success in recent years with sports utility vehicles (SUVs). When SUVs were first introduced, most manufacturers produced one mid-sized model, such as the Chevy Blazer or Ford Explorer. As the popularity of SUVs grew, the manufacturers began to appeal to other market segments with smaller-sized models, such as the Toyota RAV4, and then very large models, including the Mercury Mountaineer and Cadillac Escalade. Some companies offer only one of those model sizes, while others have a model in each size category for a full product line.

Another way of developing a product line is to offer differences in quality and price. If you visit an appliance store, you will usually find low-, mid-, and high-priced choices for each type of appliance, such as refrigerators, dishwashers, and microwaves. The price differences are based on the construction, quality of materials, and available features and options. A person buying a microwave for a college dorm room probably does not want the most expensive, full-featured choices, and so will be drawn to the low-price level of the product line. On the other hand, a gourmet chef making a purchase for a new kitchen may want only the highest quality and latest features.

Once a company has made decisions about a product line, it should then continue planning by determining the product assortment. A **product assortment** is the complete set of all products a business offers to a market. A product assortment can have depth, breadth, or both. A company offering a deep product assortment carries a large number of choices of features for each product category it handles. Walk into a Bath and Body Works store and look at the variety of fragrances, colors, bottle sizes, and packages for any of the major products sold there. That is an example of a deep assortment. Compare that to the choices of bath lotions that you might find in a small drug store, where the assortment would be limited.

A broad product assortment means that a business offers a large number of different but often related products for their customers. If you visit a garden center, you may find many different types of products for lawns and gardens ranging from plants, shrubs, and trees, to lawn mowers, hoses, and patio furniture. While there may not be many choices within one of the product categories, the customers should be able to meet most of their outdoor home needs at one location. As shown in Figure 22-1, businesses can choose any combination of depth and breadth of their product assortment. Some will be very small and specialized, while others will offer a complete variety of many different products.

■ PACKAGING

Two important product mix decisions are packaging and branding. While neither decision is directly related to the actual physical product itself, each can be an important influence on purchase decisions.

Most companies package their products before selling them. The package can serve four different purposes. First, it protects the product while it is being shipped and stored. Products can easily be damaged when they are grouped together for shipment from the factory to the retail store. Boxes and containers are needed for protection. The actual

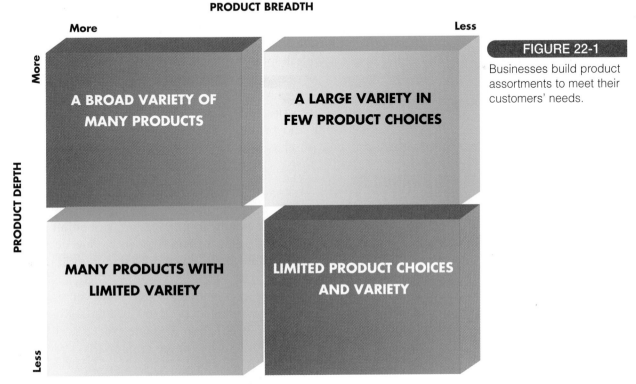

PRODUCT BREADTH

More — Less

PRODUCT DEPTH (More — Less)

A BROAD VARIETY OF MANY PRODUCTS

A LARGE VARIETY IN FEW PRODUCT CHOICES

MANY PRODUCTS WITH LIMITED VARIETY

LIMITED PRODUCT CHOICES AND VARIETY

FIGURE 22-1

Businesses build product assortments to meet their customers' needs.

ILLUSTRATION 22-2

What different purposes could the packaging of this product serve?

container or wrapping in which the individual product is packaged also offers protection on the store shelf and even can offer security to keep the product from being lost or stolen.

Second, the package can provide important information to customers on product composition, special features, and proper use. Boxes and containers also provide information to shippers on appropriate handling, storage, and delivery.

A package can be designed to make the product easier to use. Soda pop in a plastic bottle is less likely to be broken if dropped. An easy-opening lid or a container design that fits the hands of the consumer makes product handling easier. Window cleaner that is premixed in a spray bottle is much more convenient than one that requires the consumer to pour the cleaner in a bucket and apply it with a sponge.

Finally, especially for consumer products, the package is often an important promotional tool. A well-designed, attractive package calls attention to itself on the store shelf, helps the customer recall previously seen advertising, and provides a reminder of the needs that the product will satisfy if purchased.

■ BRANDING

Can you name the brands of clothing, pizza, and toothpaste you prefer? Do you and your friends regularly shop at certain stores but not others? Product and store brands play a major role in buying decisions. A **brand** is a name, symbol, word, or design that identifies a product, service, or company.

Why are brands so important to consumers? Have you ever shopped in a store that had generic (non-branded) products or that sold only unfamiliar brands? Without any information to guide you, it is difficult to make a product selection with which you are comfortable. You and people you trust have had experiences with various brands. If you find

FACTS AND FIGURES

"Corporate identity" refers to a company's name or logo—its visual expression or its "look." "Corporate image" is the public's perception of a company. "Corporate branding," by contrast, is a business process—one that is planned, strategically focused, and integrated throughout the organization.

a company's products consistently meet your needs, you will likely buy from that company again. However, a negative experience will usually result in avoiding a similar purchase. If you are satisfied with one product from a company, you are likely to have confidence in a different product sold under the same brand. Businesses recognize that brand recognition is an important influence in increasing sales. The levels of consumer brand awareness are shown in Figure 22-2.

■ PURPOSES OF DISTRIBUTION

Our economic system relies on the successful exchange of products and services between businesses and consumers. But no matter how good a product is, this exchange will not occur successfully unless the company fills orders correctly and delivers the product undamaged and on time to the correct locations. These functions are all part of effective distribution. Successful exchanges are not easy. In fact, most of the problems consumers and businesses face in our economy occur during the exchange process.

Economic discrepancies are differences between the business's offerings and the consumer's requirements. Marketers are concerned about four important economic discrepancies:

1. Differences between *types* of products produced and the *types* consumers want.

2. Differences between the *quantities* produced and the *quantities* consumers want.

3. Differences between the *location* where products are produced and the *location* where consumers want them.

4. Differences between the *time* of production and the *time* consumers want the products.

Producers manufacture large quantities of one or a very few products; consumers want small quantities of a variety of products. Producers

- **Consumers are unable to identify the brand.**
- **Consumers can identify the brand but it has little influence on their purchase decision.**
- **Consumers can identify the brand but will not purchase it because of its brand.**
- **Consumers easily recognize the brand and will choose it if it is available.**
- **Consumers view the brand as the most satisfying and will not purchase a different brand.**

FIGURE 22-2

The Five Levels of Consumer Brand Awareness

manufacture products at a specific time and in a particular location; that time and location do not typically match the place and time consumers need the product. Distribution systems are designed to get the types and quantities of products customers want to the locations where and when they want them.

■ CHANNELS OF DISTRIBUTION

The routes products follow while moving from the producer to the consumer, including all related activities and participating organizations, are called **channels of distribution.** Businesses that participate in activities that transfer goods and services from the producer to the user are called **channel members**.

Channel members are generally retailers and wholesalers. As you learned in Chapter 21, a retailer sells directly to the consumer. A wholesaler, on the other hand, buys from and sells to other businesses or organizations rather than to final consumers. Wholesalers, retailers, and other channel members serve important and specific roles in the exchange process.

Determining the number and type of businesses and the activities they will perform in a channel of distribution is an important decision. Adding businesses to the channel makes the channel more complex and difficult to control. However, using businesses that have particular expertise in transportation, product handling, or other distribution activities may result in improved distribution or actual cost savings. The activities that need to be performed as a product moves from producer to consumer will help to determine the number and types of businesses in the channel.

Customers influence the development of a distribution channel. When developing a channel, businesses must consider the location of customers, the number of customers wanting the product, and the ways in which customers prefer to purchase and consume the products.

Producers need distribution channels whether they make products for consumers or for other businesses. The channels that products follow may be quite simple and short or long and complex. The shortest path is for the producer to sell directly to the user; the longest path can include a retailer, a wholesaler, and even other businesses.

When producers sell directly to the ultimate consumer, it is called **direct distribution.** When distribution takes place through channel members, it is called **indirect distribution.** Figure 22-3 illustrates different types of distribution channels.

■ DIRECT DISTRIBUTION

Direct distribution (sometimes called *direct marketing*) is accomplished in a number of ways. One way is for sales representatives to call on users in person. This is the primary method businesses use when sell-

DIRECT DISTRIBUTION

INDIRECT DISTRIBUTION

PRODUCER — PRODUCER — PRODUCER

WHOLESALER

RETAILER — RETAILER

CONSUMER — CONSUMER — CONSUMER

FIGURE 22-3

Types of Distribution Channels for Consumer Products

ing to other businesses. Another popular form of direct distribution is the use of the mail. Businesses send letters and advertising brochures or catalogs to prospective customers through the mail or e-mail. Customers can use a mail-order form, telephone, fax, or an online order form to make purchases directly from the manufacturer.

Today, one of the most popular methods of direct distribution is telemarketing. **Telemarketing** is marketing goods and services by telephone. It combines telephone sales with computer technology. Salespeople at computer terminals make and receive calls to and from prospective customers. Some telemarketing simply involves taking orders from customers who have seen merchandise advertised on television or through direct-mail advertising. When making a sale, the salesperson completes an order form displayed on the terminal screen. Then the salesperson routes the form to the company's distribution center for shipment. Telemarketing is an extremely efficient method of direct marketing, although its misuse by some consumer marketing companies has given it a bad name. Poorly prepared salespeople and calls placed at an inconvenient time for products that customers don't want are not effective business practices.

An increasingly popular method of direct

— Exam 2
? 4

ILLUSTRATION 22-3

What are some of the positive and negative aspects of telemarketing?

ETHICAL ISSUES

TELEMARKETING—DOING IT RIGHT!

Telemarketing employs more people in the U.S. than any other form of direct marketing. Over 1 million people work directly in telemarketing, and their work creates over 8 million additional jobs in order processing, distribution, and related support positions. Companies spent $58 billion on telemarketing in the late 1990s compared to $37 billion on direct mail. However, telemarketing often has a negative image. Telemarketers sometimes bother people, act rude or unprepared, or mislead customers into thinking they are participating in a survey.

The responsibility for ethical business practices is shared by individual businesses, professional business associations, federal and state governments, consumer groups, and individual consumers. Each is responsible for enforcing laws and regulations when companies violate established fair business practices.

Business associations create codes of ethics that, while not enforceable by law, provide guidelines for ethical practices for member businesses. The association enforces the code of ethics by publicizing the information to consumers, asking customers to identify unethical businesses, and removing businesses from the association if they violate the code.

Here are some key features of the American Teleservices Association Code of Ethics for Telemarketing:

- Companies should not call people who are unlikely to be interested.
- Calls should be monitored by the company to ensure quality service.
- The product and delivery should be exactly as promised, and consumers should be informed of their options if service is unsatisfactory.
- All calls should clearly identify the name of the organization making the call and the purpose of the call.
- Guarantees and warranties should be clearly disclosed and copies made available on request.
- Merchandise should not be sent without clear customer permission.
- All calls should be made during reasonable hours.

THINK CRITICALLY

1. Why do you believe telemarketing is such a successful direct marketing tool yet continues to receive a large number of consumer complaints?
2. Based on your experience with telemarketing, do telemarketers generally follow the ethics statements listed above? Which are most often followed and which are not?
3. What responsibilities do you believe consumers have in dealing with ethical problems they encounter with telemarketing? Should they do anything when they encounter ethical treatment from businesses?
4. Prepare several statements of ethical practices that should apply to Internet marketing.

Source: *www.ataconnect.org (The American Teleservices Association, Inc.); www.the-dma.org (Direct Marketing Association's Telephone Marketing guidelines)*

distribution is through the Internet. A manufacturer can develop a Web site on which to feature its products. Customers order the products online from the site, and the company ships the products directly to the purchaser. Internet sales are expected to become a large part of sales for many companies because of the speed and efficiency of this distribution method.

▇ INDIRECT DISTRIBUTION

When producers cannot or choose not to perform all marketing activities, they need an indirect channel of distribution. Manufacturers can simplify many of their marketing operations by selling to retailers. They will need fewer salespeople, because they sell to a small number of retail customers rather than to a very large number of final consumers. They can share advertising with the retailers, and the retailers will be responsible for much of the product storage, consumer credit management, and other activities. Retailers specialize in marketing activities, and this allows producers to specialize in manufacturing activities. As you learned in Chapter 1, specialization leads to improved efficiency, which benefits consumers through lower prices and added or improved services.

Retailers benefit consumers in several ways. Unlike producers, retailers can be conveniently located near consumers and can provide the products of many manufacturers in one place, thereby permitting consumers to make comparisons among a variety of types and brands of products. Furthermore, retailers can offer several kinds of products that consumers may need, making it possible for consumers to do all their shopping at one or a few locations. Retailers offer convenient shopping hours, credit terms, merchandise exchanges, and other special services to encourage customers to shop in their businesses.

Retail businesses range from large department stores that stock a broad variety of merchandise to small retailers specializing in a limited variety. Also, there is a growing number of non-store retailers. They sell products to customers in a number of ways that do not require a shopping trip to a store. Those ways include vending machines; direct marketing by retailers through telephone, catalog, or computer-ordering services; in-home parties and sales presentations; and shopping channels on cable television.

Producers prefer to sell products to retailers that buy in large quantities, such as department and discount stores and supermarkets. Smaller retailers are usually not able to deal directly with the manufacturer, so they must buy from other channel members. They turn to wholesalers, who consolidate the orders of a number of smaller businesses and then place the larger orders with manufacturers.

Wholesalers provide valuable services that producers may not provide. They sell to retailers in small quantities and can usually deliver goods quickly. Also, many wholesalers offer credit terms to retailers and provide help in planning promotions and sales strategies.

Wholesalers sell business products as well as consumer products. Many small businesses cannot purchase in the quantities required by large manufacturers or meet their terms of sale. These small businesses seek the service of a wholesaler, often called an *industrial distributor*, to purchase the products they need.

Wholesalers are an important part of international marketing today. Those that have developed international customers and distribution systems offer an effective way for companies to enter those markets. International wholesalers can also import products from other countries to sell to their customers.

■ INTEGRATED MARKETING CHANNELS

Usually the businesses involved in a channel of distribution are independent businesses. Those businesses make their own decisions and provide the activities they believe their customers want. It is not unusual for businesses in a distribution channel to have conflicts with each other. One of the challenges in distribution planning is to develop cooperative relationships among channel members.

One of the ways for channels to work more effectively is for a large business in the channel to take responsibility for planning, coordination, and communication. The business organizes the channel so that each participant will benefit and helps the other businesses complete their responsibilities successfully. A channel in which one organization takes a leadership position to benefit all channel members is known as an **administered channel**.

Cooperation is difficult among businesses that operate at different levels of a channel and have very different responsibilities. Some very large businesses attempt to solve that problem through channel integration. **Channel integration** occurs when one business owns the organizations at other levels of the channel. A manufacturer may purchase the businesses that provide wholesaling or retailing functions. A large retailer may decide to buy a wholesaler or even several small manufacturing businesses. Each business can still provide the specific functions needed for a successful channel, but having one owner for all businesses avoids the conflicts that occur in other channels.

■ DEVELOPING A CHANNEL OF DISTRIBUTION

From the available channels of distribution ranging from direct and simple to indirect and complex, producers must decide which channel or channels will best fit their needs. Producers generally prefer to use as few channels and channel members as possible. Sometimes producers need to use more than one channel to get the widest distribution for their product. Products such as books, candy, pens, and soap are purchased by many people in a variety of locations. Such items will require several channels to reach all of the possible consumers. The manufacturers may sell directly to national discount stores that can sell large quantities of the product. To reach other markets, the manufacturers may sell to large wholesalers that, in turn, sell to supermarkets, convenience stores, vendors, or other types of businesses.

Selling to different types of customers will result in varied channels of distribution. For example, a magazine publisher may sell magazines through retail stores, news agencies, newsstands, and magazine subscription agencies, as well as directly through the mail or Internet to subscribers. Figure 22-4 summarizes these different channels.

Producers must consider many factors when deciding which channel or channels to select for distributing the company's products. Some of the main factors are:

1. *Perishability of the product.* Highly perishable articles require rapid and careful handling. Those products, such as bread, fresh flowers, and ice cream, are usually marketed directly to the consumer or through very few channel members.

2. *Geographic distance between producer and consumer.* Many products are now sold internationally as well as throughout the country in which they are produced. If the market is very close to the point of production, there is less need for channel members. More businesses will likely participate in handling a product as the distance from producer to consumer increases.

3. *Need for special handling of the product.* If the product requires costly procedures or equipment for handling, it is likely to pass through as few channel members as possible. Gasoline, which requires pipelines, special tanks, and trucks for handling, is moved from the refiner to the retailer as directly as possible. Refiners own some gasoline retail outlets. Products that are highly complex and need experts to install

FIGURE 22-4

Five Possible Channels for the Sale of Magazines to Consumers

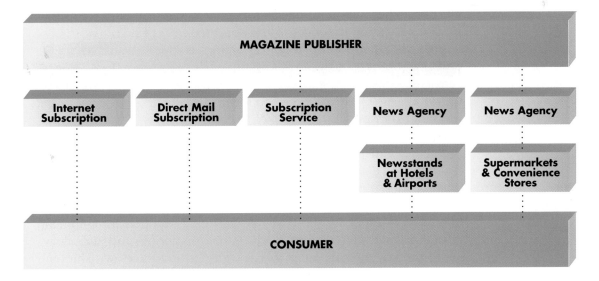

and repair also require short channels. Manufacturers of large computer systems, for example, sell directly to users.

4. *Number of users.* The greater the number of users of a product, the more channel members there probably will be. For instance, the manufacturer of steel is likely to sell directly to a few large users, whereas a shoe manufacturer may sell to wholesalers that then distribute to a variety of retail businesses.

5. *Number of types of products manufactured.* A producer that has only one product, such as pottery, will probably sell to a wholesaler. It is too expensive to maintain a sales force large enough to contact all retailers in the country. But if a producer has a large number of electrical products, such as coffee makers, clocks, heaters, and toasters, it might sell directly to large retailers that handle all of these products. The marketing costs can be distributed over many products.

6. *Financial strength and interests of the producer.* Large companies that are strong financially are better able to perform the marketing activities required to move goods from producer to consumer through the least number of channel members. They may find it more profitable to handle the marketing activities within the company rather than using other businesses. It also gives them more control over the channel rather than relying on others to perform many of the activities.

Channel decisions, like other marketing decisions, require careful study and are subject to change. Changes in technology, in transportation and storage facilities, and in retail methods are reasons why producers are constantly looking for more efficient ways to market their goods.

■ TRANSPORTATION DECISIONS

Selecting the channel members that will help sell the product to the consumer is only one of the distribution decisions a company must make. Another important decision is how to physically transport the products from the producer to the consumer.

Buyers and sellers face several common problems related to transportation. One problem deals with the types of products to be shipped. Factors to consider in shipping include the size, shape, and weight of the goods. Also, certain goods are fragile and may need special care in handling. Transporting 100 tons of steel, for example, requires much different treatment from that required for moving a carton of glassware.

Another transportation problem is the time needed for delivery. Some buyers expect or need shipment within a matter of hours, and others may not need or expect delivery for several weeks. Still another shipping problem is cost. In addition to the basic transportation charges, there are the costs of packaging products for shipment, insurance, and often storing products before, during, and after delivery to the buyer. Companies that do not perform their own shipping activities must first decide on their products' distribution requirements.

Then they can select the transportation method and companies that can meet these requirements.

Both consumers and business people are concerned about the quality of products at the time of purchase. They also want to have products available where and when they need them and at a reasonable cost. Since distribution activities affect all of these concerns, businesses plan them carefully.

■ COMMON TRANSPORTATION METHODS

The most commonly used methods of transporting goods are by railroad, truck, and airplane. A business may use more than one type of transportation, depending on the requirements for the shipment.

Railway transportation is one of the most common forms of shipping in the United States. Over a third of the volume of products shipped in the U.S. go by rail car. The principal advantage of rail transportation is low cost for moving heavy and bulky items long distances. However, products move slowly on long train routes because of the need to drop off cars that have arrived at their destination or are being routed in another direction or to add cars to the train. For bulky products or for shipping large quantities, the cost of shipping by rail is usually lower than for other methods.

Trucks are frequently used for short-distance shipping. Trucks are essential to smaller communities and rural areas that other transportation methods do not serve. Industries such as agriculture, mining, and lumber depend on trucks to move products from the source of production to the location of processing.

Much long-distance shipping is also done by truck. For products that need to be moved rapidly, in smaller quantities than can be economically shipped by rail, or where rail is not accessible, trucks are the typical transportation choice. Some transportation companies load truck trailers and place them on railroad cars to be shipped close to the final destination. This service is called **piggyback service.** Many trucking companies are now using computer systems to track customer orders and reroute trucks for rapid pickup and delivery. This flexibility is important for businesses that are trying to keep inventories low while maintaining high service levels.

Airplanes provide the most rapid form of transportation, but their rates are much higher than other methods. Airplanes can move products quickly over long distances. Items can move across a country in a few hours and around the world in a day, if necessary. The majority of air shipments involve items of relatively small bulk, high value, or quick perishability. Packages and mail are moved regularly on passenger airlines as well as through air parcel companies. Airlines are also used for shipping cut flowers, high-fashion clothing, seafood, film, and jewelry. Air shipments are very important for items needed in emergencies, such as medicine and blood, parts for machines needing quick repairs, or important documents.

United Parcel Service is the world's largest package distribution company. It transports more than 3 billion parcels and documents annually. The company uses more than 500 aircraft, 149,000 vehicles, and 1,700 facilities to provide service in more than 200 countries and territories.

Increasingly, businesses are shipping large and bulky items on special cargo planes. The planes have been designed for easy loading and unloading. Regional air freight terminals are being constructed so products can be moved rapidly into and out of airports without interfering with passenger travel. As rapid and efficient transportation becomes more important to businesses and consumers, more products are being shipped by air, even though the cost is higher. People pay more for the transportation that meets their requirements.

■ OTHER TRANSPORTATION METHODS

Water transportation (ocean, lake, and river) is the slowest method of transporting goods. However, it is also the cheapest for bulky goods, such as coal, iron ore, oil, lumber, grain, and cotton. Those are the principal items transported by water. Many products that are produced in large volume for international markets, such as automobiles and large pieces of equipment, are shipped across the oceans. At any large harbor on a coast you can see hundreds of types of products being loaded and unloaded from ships.

In the U.S., as well as in many other countries, networks of thousands of miles of pipelines have been built. Pipelines mostly transport petroleum and natural gas. In many countries, however, pipelines are important methods of moving water for irrigation and for human consumption.

One way of improving shipping services is through **containerization.** Products are packed in large shipping containers at the factory and are then shipped using a number of transportation methods before being unpacked. The containers can easily be loaded and unloaded from trucks to rail cars, ships, and cargo planes, and back to trucks. This reduces the amount of product handling and product damage.

ILLUSTRATION 22-4

How could containerization improve shipping services?

◼ PRODUCT HANDLING

Lost, late, or damaged products are of little value to customers. Product handling is an important part of the distribution process. Most products are handled several times on their way from producer to consumer. Each time a product is handled adds to the cost of distribution, increases delivery time, and increases the opportunity for damage to occur. Businesses evaluate their product-handling procedures to find ways to improve the process. Improvements may include more secure packaging, more efficient procedures for packing and unpacking, and better equipment for handling and storing products.

◼ TRACKING PRODUCTS

An important part of product handling is keeping track of the products. Businesses and customers want to know where products are in the distribution channel and when they will be delivered. The record keeping required is often a very time-consuming task. Businesses now use bar coding to track products during distribution. **Bar codes** are product identification labels containing a unique set of vertical bars that computer scanning equipment can read. Each product or container has a bar code. The scanning equipment can read the codes at any time during distribution to track the product's progress.

— Exam2 ?3

◼ PRODUCT STORAGE

Manufacturers or channel members often must store products at points along the way from producer to consumer. Usually, consumers do not buy products as soon as they are produced. Producers and channel members may want to accumulate a large quantity of products to make shipping more efficient. Also, consumers buy some products more during one time of the year than another. Lawn mowers, air conditioners, snowmobiles, and skis are examples of such products. Most companies

ILLUSTRATION 22-5

How are bar codes used in product handling?

produce those products throughout the year to make production more efficient. They then store the products until they are ready to distribute them for sale.

Warehouses are buildings used to store large quantities of products until they can be sold. They are usually large buildings with racks, shelves, or bins for storing products. Warehouse operators may control temperature or humidity if the stored products need special protection. They must carefully handle and store the products to prevent damage. Warehouse personnel keep computerized records of where each product is stored in the warehouse. When they receive an order, the computer displays the quantity of the product available and its location in the warehouse.

Handling products and storing them for a long time is expensive. Also, moving them around increases the chances for damage. For more efficient handling with less risk of damage, many companies now use mechanical equipment and robots to handle the products in their warehouses. Computers control both the equipment and the robots as products are moved into storage and subsequently removed for shipment.

Large wholesalers and retailers that handle a variety of products and sell them through a number of outlets have replaced traditional warehouses with distribution centers. A **distribution center** is a large building designed to accumulate and redistribute products efficiently. A wholesaler or retailer usually buys products from a number of manufacturers. Each manufacturer ships these products to the distribution center in large quantities. Center workers then repackage the products into smaller quantities, combine them with products from other manufacturers, and ship them to stores that sell that bundle of products to consumers. Distribution centers can save businesses a great deal of money. They reduce transportation and storage costs and provide individual stores with the products they need quickly. Individual stores can order smaller quantities than if they had to order merchandise from each manufacturer, so products will not become outdated as easily.

■ ORDER PROCESSING

Customers place orders in person or by mail, telephone, computer, or fax machine. When an order reaches the business, employees must process the paperwork to fill the order and bill the customer. If customers have questions or problems with the order, employees must handle them in a friendly and courteous fashion. Some employees are responsible for tracking the order until it reaches the customers to make sure the customers receive what they expect.

Most companies have now automated some or all of the order processing system. Orders entered into a computer system can be easily tracked. Some companies now make computer records available to channel members and customers, so they can also track orders at any time from their own computers.

CHAPTER CONCEPTS

■ Businesses think of their products as what they have to offer to consumers. Consumers are more likely to think of products as ways to satisfy their needs.

■ Businesses develop products on three levels: a basic product, enhanced product, and extended product. Also, businesses must decide whether to offer product lines and product assortments.

■ Packaging adds value by protecting the product during shipping and storage; providing information about product composition, features, use, and proper handling; making the product easier to use; and promoting the product.

■ Branding gives customers confidence in making a purchase. If they recognize a brand name and have had good experiences with that brand, they will be more likely to buy the brand again.

■ Effective distribution gets the correct products to customers at the right place and time and in the correct form.

■ Channels of distribution can be either direct (from manufacturer directly to the purchaser) or indirect (using retailers and sometimes wholesalers to handle some of the marketing activities). Distribution activities include product handling and storing, transporting and tracking the product, order processing, and customer service.

BUILD VOCABULARY POWER

Define the following terms and concepts.

1. basic product
2. enhanced product
3. extended product
4. product line
5. product assortment
6. brand
7. economic discrepancies
8. channels of distribution
9. channel members
10. direct distribution
11. indirect distribution
12. telemarketing
13. administered channel
14. channel integration
15. piggyback service
16. containerization
17. bar codes
18. warehouses
19. distribution centers

REVIEW FACTS

1. What is likely to happen to consumers and to the business if the business makes poor product development decisions? What effect do good development decisions have?
2. How does the consumer's view of a product differ from the business's view?
3. What is the difference between a warranty and a guarantee?
4. Why would a company want to offer differences in product quality and price as part of a product line?
5. What are several different purposes of product packaging?

6. How does a brand name help consumers make decisions about the products they plan to purchase?
7. What are the five levels of consumer brand awareness?
8. What are some examples of economic discrepancies that occur between producers and consumers?
9. Provide several examples of direct distribution.
10. List several benefits to businesses and consumers of using indirect distribution.
11. What are several important factors that producers should consider when selecting the channels of distribution to use for a product?
12. Provide an example of how timing and cost of shipping can affect the transportation method selected to distribute a product.
13. For each of the three commonly used transportation methods, describe a type of product that would most likely be shipped by each method.
14. Why is careful product handling important to both businesses and consumers?
15. In what ways can technology improve product handling?
16. What tasks do customer service employees perform after receiving a customer's order?

DISCUSS IDEAS

1. If a company believes in the marketing concept, it will try to provide products and services that its target market needs. Does that mean the company will not have to offer as many enhanced and extended products? Why or why not?
2. Identify a company with a product that has an extensive product line. Identify specific products that are part of the product line. Then describe the differences among those products and why they meet different customers' needs.
3. For a product with which you are familiar, describe ways that the packaging improves sales and usability. Now identify examples of packaging that interferes with sales and usability.
4. What are some reasons why consumers may reject a specific brand, even though they are very familiar with it?
5. Three producers make the same type and quality of cosmetics for sale. Producer A sells through wholesalers to retailers. Producer B sells directly to retailers. Producer C sells through door-to-door sales representatives. Why might the selling price be about the same, even though the channels of distribution are different?
6. Provide examples showing that the ways in which consumers purchase a product influence the type of distribution channel used.
7. Why might a manufacturer choose to sell products through a department store rather than a discount store?
8. Why would a company use a truck to haul products from the East Coast to the West Coast when railroad shipping is cheaper?

9. Make a list of products you purchased that were probably stored for a length of time before you purchased them. Then make a similar list of products that were not stored or were stored only a short time before you purchased them. Discuss the differences among the products.

10. Discuss the problems businesses and consumers might encounter with product distribution and order processing when the Internet is used for selling and buying.

ANALYZE INFORMATION

1. Most people are very aware of the brands of many of the products they use, but the brands they remember best may or may not be the ones they actually purchase. Form a team with other classmates to conduct a consumer survey. As a team, prepare a questionnaire for five product categories. Include some products with very familiar brands and other products with mostly unfamiliar brands. Each team member should use the questionnaire to interview a number of people representing various ages and interests. For each product, ask the person to list the brand names that are most memorable to them. Then have them identify the brand they most often purchase or use. When the interviews are complete, compile the results into a short report and draw conclusions about the importance of branding in influencing purchases.

2. A student organization to which you belong has decided to sell containers of bottled water at after-school activities, athletic events, and other functions as a fundraiser. Your organization made an agreement with the supplier that allows you to design a unique package for the water bottle. Prepare a diagram and description of the package you would recommend that will meet the four different purposes of packaging described in the chapter.

3. Bascagio's Bakery makes cookies, cakes, and pastries that it distributes directly to retail grocers within a 60-mile area with its own trucks. The company is considering doubling its baking facilities and marketing its products over a 200-mile area.
   a. If the distribution area is going to be much wider, will the bakery have to use an indirect channel of distribution? List the advantages and disadvantages of an indirect system.
   b. What outlets, other than retail grocers, can the company use for its products?
   c. Does the number of outlets help determine whether a direct or indirect channel is better? Explain.

4. An appliance store can purchase a certain brand of electric heater for $45.00 from a firm in City A or for $48.50 from another firm in City B. The transportation cost from City A is $3.88 per heater.

From City B, the transportation cost is $2.77 per heater. What is the difference in the cost of the purchase from each firm if the appliance store buys 500 heaters? What factors other than cost should the appliance store consider when deciding from which firm to make the purchase?

5. A company located in Utah manufactures children's toys and games. Its potential customers are located throughout the world. Identify ways in which it can use each of the following distribution methods to improve its customer service or profitability: (a) Internet sales, (b) containerization, (c) bar coding.

SOLVE BUSINESS PROBLEMS

CASE 22-1

Albany Muran has been a part-time photographer for many years. She has emphasized individual family portraits for most of her business. She primarily gets customers through word-of-mouth from people who see her portraits in people's homes. She enjoys the work but doesn't make enough money to do it full time. She has discussed the issue with several business advisors, who advised her to consider expanding beyond portrait photography. They recommended expanding into weddings and special events; taking photos of landscapes, buildings, animals, and such that would meet the needs of a broader audience; or purchasing and reselling home accessories that would comple-

ment the purchase of pictures and portraits. She is unsure of what direction to take with her business.

Think Critically:

1. Describe a basic product, enhanced product, and extended products that you would recommend to Albany for expanding her business.
2. If Albany decided to purchase and resell home accessories, how could she use the concept of a product line to effectively market those products?
3. Construct a grid like the one shown in Figure 22-1 for Albany, illustrating how she could develop a business that would fit into each of the four quadrants. Make sure to describe the types of products she would offer for each of the four positions on the grid.

CASE 22-2

The Elegant Affair is a specialty retail shop. It sells assorted gift boxes of various meats, cheeses, nuts, jams, and jellies. The business is located in a Midwest city and is facing declining sales due to the city's economic difficulties. One major manufacturing plant has closed, and layoffs from other businesses have caused many people to move from the area seeking new jobs.

The president of the company has been studying telemarketing as a way to increase sales without having to move the store or build a new store in an area with a more attractive economic climate. She believes that by using salespeople and a computerized telemarketing system, the company can sell the gift boxes to people throughout the U.S. She also believes that the cost of those sales will actually be lower than selling the products to people who come into the store.

Think Critically:

1. What types of activities would The Elegant Affair have to do to start a telemarketing system?
2. How can the company identify prospective customers in order for the telemarketing salespeople to call them?
3. Identify two distribution methods that The Elegant Affair might use for the products it sells through telemarketing. What are the advantages and disadvantages of each?
4. Develop a brief script for the telemarketing salespeople to use to introduce the company and its products to prospective customers.
5. Do you believe an online alternative for customer ordering might be a better method for the company than telemarketing? Why or why not?

PROJECT: MY BUSINESS, INC.

Two important marketing decisions for your new business are the type and assortment of products you will offer and how to distribute the products. Some new businesses have very limited product choices, while others offer an extensive set of enhanced and extended products. Most retail businesses purchase products and supplies from other channel members, so they are part of an indirect channel of distribution. An important part of distribution is to select a good location for the business that makes it convenient for customers to find the business and purchase your product. In this project segment, you will study the product development and distribution decisions for your new juice business.

DATA COLLECTION

1. Identify your basic physical product. Remember that it will be very similar to that offered by many competitors. Then study as many competitors as you can and identify the possible extended and enhanced product choices for this type of business.

2. Again, by studying competitors and collecting additional information about this type of business from magazines and the Internet, list possible product lines that seem appropriate for the juice products. Also identify possible product assortments.

3. Collect examples of the packages and brand names used by the primary competitors selling these products in your community.

4. Develop a simple map of the area of your town or city where you might locate your new business. Mark on the map the locations of the businesses that offer the same types of products you are considering.

ANALYSIS

1. Given your understanding of product development and the information you collected, develop a product strategy that identifies the products, product lines, and product assortments you plan to offer during your first six months in operation. Justify your choices.

2. Prepare a sales presentation on your products. Videotape it or present it to your class.

3. Review a business directory from your community or on the Internet. Identify at least four manufacturers or suppliers from whom you might purchase the products and supplies you will need for your business.

4. Design the basic juice cup or container you will use to package your product. If possible, contact a supplier and determine the cost of various sizes of cup or container. Identify any other packaging you will need.

5. Using the map you prepared in the Data Collection section of this activity, identify the three locations you prefer for your new business. Make sure that retail businesses can actually be located there. Rank your preferred locations with a short rationale for your decisions. What kind of image will you want your facility to convey?

6. Once your facility has been determined, analyze any immediate and long-term improvements needed for the facility.

7. Develop a distribution plan. Include the methods you plan to use to store products and supplies and transport them to your stores. Also list other possible channels for distributing your products.

PRICING AND PROMOTION

OBJECTIVES

23-1 Discuss how businesses and consumers make their buying decisions.

23-2 Describe factors involved in establishing product prices and common pricing strategies.

23-3 Discuss ways that companies try to control costs that can lead to higher prices.

23-4 Discuss the purpose of promotion in meeting business and consumer needs.

23-5 Identify common promotional methods.

23-6 Explain the parts of the selling process and how each is used to help customers make effective buying decisions.

23-7 Identify important laws and regulations that apply to advertising and promotion.

WHY PAY MORE?

ichi and Arturo walked out of Windzors, a sporting goods store that had just opened in the new Regency Park shopping plaza. "I can't believe that store will be successful," said Michi. "I've never seen sports equipment priced that high!"

"The products really were expensive," agreed Arturo. "But it certainly isn't a normal sporting goods store. The salesperson said they would help design your own set of personalized golf clubs and that you would get five hours of lessons with the golf pro at the Regency Sports Centre if you purchased a set of clubs."

"Did you see the area where they sold downhill skis?" asked Michi. "They had a moving slide like an escalator where you could actually ski.

They also had a machine that formed molds around your feet for custom-fitting ski boots. They sponsor a ski club and organize vacations to the mountains in the United States and even to other countries. I've never seen that in a sporting goods store."

"Why would people want to pay that much?" Arturo wondered. "Sure, they have the top brand names and unique services. But you can get the same type of products for 40 to 50 percent less at other stores."

"I don't know," said Michi. "They certainly have effective advertising, sales brochures, and customer service. And the store was filled with people. Maybe the owners are on to something."

A business is successful when it brings buyers and sellers together, and they are both satisfied with the exchange. To be successful, businesses must offer the type and quality of products and services that meet the needs of their customers. The products must be priced so that buyers consider them a good value for the money.

Whether the buyers are businesses purchasing raw materials to use in manufacturing, equipment to operate the business, or products for resale, or consumers buying products for their own use, they must have information to make their decisions. Buyers must be aware of the products, how the products will meet their needs, and where they can buy them. Then buyers and sellers must agree on a price and method of payment. In this chapter, you will learn about the last two elements of the marketing mix: pricing and promotion.

■ THE BUSINESS BUYING DECISION

When planning a purchase, businesses actually make several specific decisions. They must decide what to purchase, when to purchase, from whom to purchase, and how much to purchase.

■ WHAT TO PURCHASE

To be successful, a business must keep the right kind of products in stock. Manufacturers buy products to use in producing products to sell to their customers. Wholesale or retail businesses purchase products for resale or for use in the operation of their businesses. In all

ILLUSTRATION 23-1

When planning a purchase, what decisions do businesses typically make?

cases, the most important consideration in making purchases is their customers' needs. Businesses that do not satisfy customers will not thrive. Businesses must consider both quality and assortment of products in deciding what to purchase.

Some buyers try to sell more products than their competitors by offering low-quality products at a low price. They believe that price is so important to customers that the customers will accept lower quality in order to save money. This strategy can backfire. Customers compare price and quality to make the best possible decision. They will usually not select the absolute cheapest product if it is of inferior quality nor will they always pay the highest price even if quality is superior.

Two factors influence a business's selection of product assortment. The first is competition. A new store will have a hard time attracting customers if it carries only the same products or brands that are carried by local businesses that are already successful. A business needs to emphasize the products customers want but offer some differences from competitors' products.

The second factor in choosing a product assortment is the financial ability of the business. It costs a great deal to keep a wide selection of products available. Businesses can stock a limited variety of products while still offering customers a good selection. Product variety is a difficult decision. Businesses need to stock items that customers want, but their budget has limits.

Businesses have several sources of assistance in determining what to purchase. Catalogs and salespeople are valuable tools. Trade associations and their publications can also help. Businesses should listen carefully to their customers in determining what to purchase. They should also review company records of previous sales and regularly study what products sell well and not so well for competitors.

WHEN TO PURCHASE

The type of products, the types and locations of suppliers, and other factors such as style and price trends influence the decision about when to purchase. For a manufacturer, raw materials and component parts must be available when needed for production, or the business will not be able to maintain its production schedule. Wholesalers and retailers need an adequate supply of products when customers want to buy. Businesses often must place orders well in advance for products to be available when their customers need them. For example, retail clothing stores often order summer fashions in January or earlier. Whether a buyer believes the prices of products will fall or rise will also influence when product orders are placed.

FROM WHOM TO PURCHASE

Part of the purchasing decision is to choose the right suppliers. Businesses consider the reputation of each supplier in such areas as dealing with customers, filling orders rapidly and exactly as requested, and providing necessary services. Other considerations are the supplier's price and credit terms.

Businesses must decide whether to make purchases from only one supplier or to spread the orders among several suppliers. Most businesses concentrate their buying among a few suppliers. This practice usually develops better relationships between the suppliers and the purchaser. Better prices, credit terms, and service are also likely to result. However, relying on one supplier leaves the purchaser vulnerable when that business experiences problems.

HOW MUCH TO PURCHASE

A business should have sufficient products available to meet customer demand. If customers cannot purchase the products they want when they want, they will go elsewhere. If a manufacturing business runs out of the necessary raw materials and parts, they must delay production.

On the other hand, if businesses have a much larger inventory than they need, they are tying up large amounts of money in inventory that they could use in other ways to make a profit. The large inventory also requires extra storage space. If businesses keep only small quantities in stock, they reduce the risk of loss from spoilage, changes in design, or changes in demand. Many suppliers are now able to fill orders quickly, making it easier for companies to carry lower quantities of many of the products they sell.

FACTS AND FIGURES

Ethics is an important issue in purchasing. A "kickback" is a payment from a vendor to a buyer for the purpose of improperly obtaining favorable treatment in the issuance of a contract or purchase order. Other actions that are considered unacceptable include the showing of excessive favoritism toward a vendor and the solicitation or acceptance of gifts from the vendor by the purchaser.

FACTS AND FIGURES

Many car buying services are available on the Internet. For example, one service will research vehicle availability, negotiate a competitive price, verify the paperwork, and assist with delivery. The price for this service? $399.

■ PAYMENT TERMS AND DISCOUNTS

Businesses establish a price at which they would like to sell a product. The original price that the seller posts on the product is the **list price.** Often, however, customers do not pay the list price. The terms of sale offered by the seller or requested by the buyer affect the actual price paid. The terms of sale identify delivery conditions, when invoices must be paid, and whether the buyer can receive credit or discounts.

The buyer may specify the requirements the seller must meet. The buyer and seller discuss those criteria and then negotiate any changes before a final decision is made. The buyer and seller will discuss price, quantity, and delivery, and agree on the terms of the sale. The supplier then receives the buyer's purchase order or contract, which details the form, quantity, and price of the products to be supplied.

■ PAYMENT TERMS

Companies that sell to other businesses often extend credit to their customers. They list their credit terms on the invoice. Invoices often state credit terms in a form such as *net 30 days,* which means that the buyer must pay in full within 30 days from the date on the invoice. Some businesses offer longer payment terms, such as net 60 days. The longer the terms, the better for the buyer, who will then have a chance to sell the goods by the time payment is due or can earn interest on the money that it otherwise would have paid to the supplier.

■ DISCOUNTS

Suppliers may offer discounts on products that their business customers purchase. **Discounts** are reductions from the price of the product to encourage customers to buy. Common types of discounts are trade, quantity, seasonal, and cash discounts. Discounts are subtracted from the list price.

A **trade discount** is a price reduction that manufacturers give to their channel partners, such as wholesalers or retailers, in exchange for additional services. For example, a manufacturer may give retailers a 30 percent discount but may give wholesalers a 45 percent discount from the list price (or 15 percent more than retailers). In this case, the manufacturer expects the wholesalers to perform additional marketing activities beyond those expected from retailers.

A **quantity discount** is a price reduction offered to customers that buy in quantities larger than a specified minimum. For example, a retail paint store that orders 200 gallons of paint from a wholesaler pays a certain price per gallon. However, the wholesaler may lower the price per gallon if the store orders at least 1,000 gallons at one time. The purpose of the discount is to encourage customers to buy in large quantities. The manufacturer can afford to sell the larger quantity for a lower price because that sale reduces the cost of inventory, the amount of

ILLUSTRATION 23-2

Why might a business offer a seasonal discount for its products?

storage space needed, the insurance costs, and the administrative costs of product handling. Quantity discounts may be based on the number of units purchased or on the dollar value of the order.

A **seasonal discount** is a price reduction offered for ordering or taking delivery of products in advance of the normal buying period. It encourages the buyer to purchase earlier than necessary or at a time when orders are normally low. An example is a discount on snowmobiles purchased in the summer. The seasonal discount is a way the manufacturer attempts to balance production and inventory levels throughout the year for products that are normally purchased at a few specific times during the year.

To encourage early payments, many businesses offer a cash discount. A **cash discount** is a price reduction given for paying by a certain date. A cash discount is usually stated as a percentage of the purchase price (for example, 2 percent). Businesses offer cash discounts with various dating and credit terms. For example, the terms of a purchase may be net 30 days with a 2 percent discount for payment within 10 days. If the invoice is dated May 1, the buyer can deduct 2 percent from the total price when paying on or before May 11. Otherwise, the buyer must pay the full amount by May 31. Businesses express terms like these in this form: 2/10, n/30.

■ COMPONENTS OF PRICE

The prices businesses charge can make the difference between success and failure of their products. Customers must view the product as a good value for the price. The price must be competitive with prices of competitors' products yet must be high enough for the business to make a profit on the sale.

The **selling price** is the actual price customers pay for the product. The selling price is determined by subtracting any discounts from the list price. Businesses often set list prices higher than the price at which they end up selling the products. To make a profit, businesses must plan for discounts when setting their list prices.

Figure 23-1 illustrates the components that marketing managers consider when setting prices. To make a profit, marketers must set prices high enough to more than cover all costs. The income remaining after deducting costs from the selling price is the net profit for that sale.

The largest cost that the price must cover is the cost of goods sold. The **cost of goods sold** is the cost to produce the product or buy it for resale. For manufacturers, the cost of goods sold is the total cost of the materials, operations, and personnel used to make the product. For wholesalers and retailers, it is the price they pay their supplier to buy the product plus the cost of transporting it to their location for resale to their customers. For example, if the invoice price of an item is $55 and the transportation charge is $5, the cost of goods sold is $60.

Operating expenses are the costs of operating a business. They do not include costs involved in the actual production or purchase of merchandise, which would be a part of the cost of goods sold. Most costs involved in the day-to-day running of a business fall into this category. Figure 23-2 lists some common operating expenses.

The **margin** or **gross profit** is the difference between the selling price and the cost of goods sold. In Figure 23-1, the margin is 40 cents. Marketers think of the margin as the percentage of sales available to cover operating expenses and provide a profit. For example, a busi-

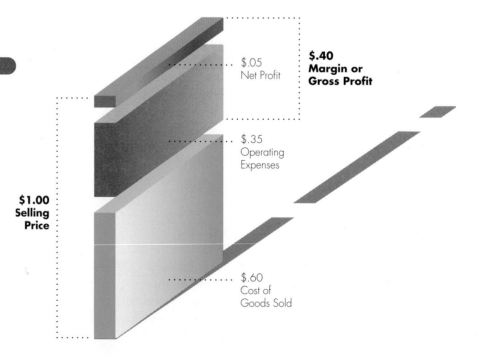

FIGURE 23-1

A product's selling price is made up of several components.

$1.00 Selling Price

$.40 Margin or Gross Profit

$.05 Net Profit

$.35 Operating Expenses

$.60 Cost of Goods Sold

Rent	Taxes
Interest paid on borrowed money	Repairs and maintenance
Salaries, wages, and benefits	Supplies
Telephone service	Inventory losses due to theft,
Depreciation expense	spoilage, or breakage
Furniture, fixtures, and equipment	Customer service expenses
Uncollected accounts and collection	Advertising
expense	Donations
Delivery costs	Utilities
Insurance	Cost of business services

FIGURE 23-2

Businesses consider operating expenses such as these when setting a product's price.

–Exam2 ? 15

ness may operate on a 25 percent margin. If operating expenses are more than 25 percent of sales, the company will lose money.

Net profit is the difference between the selling price and all costs and expenses of the business. Net profit can be calculated using the following formula:

Net profit = selling price − cost of goods sold − operating expenses

Markup is the amount added to the cost of goods sold to determine the selling price. It is similar to margin. When stated in dollars and cents, markup and margin are identical. For example, in Figure 23-1, the markup is also 40 cents. Often businesses express the markup as a percentage of the cost of goods sold or as a percentage of the selling price. Thus, the markup in Figure 23-1 is 66 2/3 percent (40 cents/60 cents) of cost. Expressed as a percentage of the selling price, it is 40 percent (40 cents/100 cents).

Some consumers confuse the markup percentage with profit. They believe that if a business has a 50 percent markup, it is making a profit of 50 percent of the selling price. However, markup must cover operating expenses. If the business with a 50 percent average markup on its products has operating expenses of 45 percent of sales, it will have a profit of 5 percent of total sales.

Markdown is any amount by which the original selling price is reduced before the item is sold. Companies use markdowns when their inventory is not selling at a satisfactory rate. Since the costs associated with the products remain the same, markdowns reduce profits, so companies want to avoid them.

■ PRICING STRATEGIES

Since businesses operate for profit, they must set prices that will entice customers to buy the products yet will still make a profit after deducting costs. Businesses can use different strategies to achieve this goal. For example, a business can establish a high price. Fewer customers will buy at a high price than a low price, but the company will make a greater gross profit per item sold. On the other hand, a business can choose to set a low price. More customers will buy at a low price than a high price, but the company will make less gross profit per item sold. In this case, the company hopes to make a satisfactory profit by selling a large number of items.

No one strategy is best in all cases. Either of these strategies can result in a satisfactory profit for the company. Consider the following example:

Business A buys a product for $500 and offers it for sale at $1,000. It sells four of these in a month, making a gross profit of $2,000:

$1,000 × 4 items = $4,000 revenue from sales
$500 × 4 items = $2,000 cost of goods sold
$4,000 revenue − $2,000 cost of goods sold = $2,000 gross profit

Business B, selling the same product, thinks it can make a better profit by setting a lower price and selling a greater quantity. It offers the item for $800. During a month, it sells six items, for a gross profit of $1,800:

$800 × 6 items = $4,800 revenue from sales
$500 × 6 items = $3,000 cost of goods sold
$4,800 − $3,000 cost of goods sold = $1,800 gross profit

In this case, Business A's strategy made the greatest profit. However, either strategy could result in the greatest profit. The challenge is to choose the strategy that works best for the situation.

While both of these companies made a gross profit, they still must deduct operating expenses to arrive at their net profit. If Business A's operating expenses are much greater than Business B's, then Business B might make the greatest net profit of the two competitors, even though its gross profit was lower.

Businesses must be careful about setting extremely high or extremely low prices. With extremely high prices, the business may not sell a sufficient quantity to yield a net profit. With extremely low prices, the business may not be able to cover its costs no matter how many products it sells. Between these two extremes is a reasonable price that satisfies customers and allows a reasonable profit. Next you will learn about some of the strategies marketing managers use for setting a reasonable price.

■ PRICING TO MEET COMPETITION

The amount of competition among companies handling similar products or services is an important factor in establishing prices. If one company has much higher prices than competitors for the same products, some of the company's customers are likely to buy from the competitors. Even similar businesses in separate locations may compete for the same customers. If prices are too high in one area, many people will travel to purchase goods or services. For example, if a service station in one neighborhood is selling a certain brand of gasoline for $1.89 a gallon and a station two miles away is selling the same brand for $1.59, customers may be willing to travel to buy where the price is lower.

ILLUSTRATION 23-3

Why has the Internet had a major effect on pricing?

The Internet has had a major impact on pricing, because it makes price comparison easy for customers. Some Web sites will search for the lowest prices for specific products. Customers who value low prices over service may buy from the lowest-priced competitor.

A business may need to offer some of its merchandise at a price that does not allow a profit because a competitor has established an even lower price. However, it is not always necessary to have a lower selling price than competitors. If a company has a loyal group of customers and offers a product with some distinct advantages, or provides services that customers want and other companies do not offer, the company may be able to charge a higher price without losing customers. Remember that the cost of providing higher-quality products or more services may be expensive, so profits may not be higher just because prices are higher. Windzors, the exclusive sporting goods store in the chapter-opening case, was relying on unique products, exclusive services, and an interesting shopping experience to justify much higher product prices.

When competition is intense, some companies may have to set some of their prices at or below the actual costs of doing business. In such a competitive situation, only the most efficient businesses make a net profit. Even when competition is not strong, if a company sets its prices too high, people will try to do without its products or find substitutes, rather than pay prices that seem to give that company an unduly large profit.

■ PRICING TO EARN A SPECIFIC PROFIT

When introducing a new product, many businesses base their selling price on a specific profit they want to make. The business first determines the costs of producing and marketing the product, and all related operating expenses. It then sets the price by adding the amount necessary to make the target profit. But even setting prices based on a target profit won't guarantee that the company will make that profit. Customers still must like the product well enough to buy it at that price. Also, competitors selling the same product might sell for less, luring away customers. In either case, the company may have to mark down its price to attract more buyers, reducing profit below its target.

PRICING BASED ON CONSUMER DEMAND

The owner of a business that carries fashion merchandise knows that at certain times the products will be in great demand, and at other times the demand will be very low. Swimsuits sell quickly early in the season, but slowly late in the season, unless the retailer greatly reduces the prices. Since a retailer cannot accurately predict the exact number of suits that it will sell, it will set a selling price at the beginning of the season that should ensure a net profit on the entire inventory of swimsuits, even though it may have to drastically reduce prices later in the season.

A manufacturer of a product that suddenly becomes popular may want to sell at a high price while the demand is great. When new competitors enter the market or customers tire of the product and the demand begins to decline, the manufacturer will need to sell the product at a much lower price.

The introduction of new products in the market presents an interesting study in price decisions. High definition televisions (HDTV) are just now coming onto the market. The few brands are priced extremely high—several thousand dollars—compared to standard televisions. Within a few years, customer demand will likely increase, many more competitors will enter the market, and prices will drop to between $1,000 and $2,000 or even lower.

PRICING TO SELL MORE PRODUCTS

Products that are priced higher usually sell more slowly than those that cost the same but are priced lower. For example, a product that cost $40 may be priced at $60, but may not sell for two months. A similar product that also cost $40 may be priced at $48 and sell in two weeks. If the second product continues to sell at that pace, the business will sell more of it and achieve a larger net profit from it for the year. The business must be careful that the lower price is high enough to cover operating costs and still contribute to profit. Otherwise, using the lower price is a poor decision. For example, if the product priced at $48 had a cost of goods sold of $40 and must cover $10 worth of operating expenses, then the business will never make a net profit on the product no matter how many it sells.

If a business has a low rate of inventory turnover, it must charge higher prices to cover the cost of the inventory and the operating expenses of the business. For instance, many items in an exclusive jewelry store may be sold and replenished at the rate of once a year or less. The jeweler, therefore, must mark the retail price of the products very high in relation to its cost in order to make a reasonable profit.

■ PRICING TO PROVIDE CUSTOMER SERVICES

A business that offers credit, free delivery, or 24-hour emergency service will have higher operating expenses than one that offers no services. Higher operating expenses require a higher selling price to yield the same net profit as that earned by a business with lower expenses. If a business's customers expect a high level of service, or if the business is using the extra service to appear different from competitors, it will have to set prices higher to achieve a profit.

■ CONTROLLING COSTS

Businesses are not always able to increase prices just because they are not making a profit. Costs of merchandise and operating expenses for the business often increase, while prices charged to customers cannot be increased due to competition. Businesses have to make careful purchasing and operating decisions to avoid unnecessary expenses. Three important areas that can affect costs are (1) markdowns, (2) damaged or stolen merchandise, and (3) merchandise returns.

■ MARKDOWNS

In many cases, businesses are forced to sell some products at lower prices than they had planned. This can happen because companies purchase products that customers do not want or go out of style. Businesses also have to sell products at lower prices when they overestimated demand and bought too many products or when competition increases or competitors lower prices.

Businesses cannot avoid markdowns totally, but they can usually control them. Careful purchasing can eliminate many markdowns. Proper product handling and marketing practices can also reduce the number of markdowns.

■ DAMAGED OR STOLEN MERCHANDISE

Some products may be damaged so much that they cannot be sold. Other products may be stolen through shoplifting or employee theft. These situations have a serious effect on profits.

Assume that a product with a selling price of $5.00 is damaged or stolen. The product cost the business $4.00, and operating expenses amounted to $.75 for each product. Expected net profit was $.25. In order to recover the cost of that one damaged or stolen product, the business will have to sell 16 more products than first planned (16 products × $.25 = $4.00). It will have to sell another three products to cover operating expenses. The business will not earn a profit on the sale of the 19 products if just one product out of 20 is damaged or stolen. To reduce the amount of damaged and stolen merchandise, companies may take actions such as employing security guards or installing surveillance cameras and training employees to handle merchandise carefully.

■ RETURNED MERCHANDISE

If customers are not satisfied with their purchases, they may return the products for a refund. This adds to expenses in two ways. If the business can resell the merchandise, it will have to sell it at a reduced price. Also, many expenses are involved in handling and reselling the returned merchandise, which increases operating expenses. Most likely, some returned merchandise cannot be resold.

To make a profit, businesses must consider their record of returned merchandise when buying and pricing merchandise. They must try to buy just the type and quality of merchandise that customers prefer in order to help reduce returns. Salespeople should be trained to sell products that customers need rather than attempting to convince customers to buy things they do not need. Offering customer service and support to help customers use the products properly and resolve their problems also reduces the amount of merchandise returned.

When managers give close attention to the three problem areas of markdowns, damaged or stolen merchandise, and returns, they can keep operating expenses at a minimum. As a result, they can maintain profits while lowering the markup percentage. In that way, both the businesses and their customers benefit.

■ PROMOTION AS MARKETING COMMUNICATION

To be successful, a business must interest people in buying its products and services. Even good products will not sell automatically. Consumers need to know the product is available and where they can purchase it. They must be able to easily see the differences among brands and determine which brand will best meet their needs.

Consumers generally follow five steps in progressing toward a purchase decision. Figure 23-3 summarizes the steps in the consumer decision-making process. While the five steps are common to all consumers, each consumer has different needs and gathers information in different ways to satisfy those needs. Some customers spend a great deal of time and consult many information sources before deciding to buy or not to buy. Other consumers might not be as careful or use the same methods. Therefore, businesses must provide appropriate infor-

PROBLEM RECOGNITION

The consumer identifies a need to satisfy or a problem to solve.

INFORMATION SEARCH

The consumer gathers information about alternative solutions for the need or problem.

ALTERNATIVE EVALUATION

The consumer weighs the options to determine which will best satisfy the need or solve the problem.

PURCHASE

If the consumer identifies a suitable and affordable choice, he or she makes the purchase.

POST-PURCHASE EVALUATION

The consumer uses the product or service and evaluates how well it met the need or solved the problem.

FIGURE 23-3

Steps in the Consumer Decision-Making Process

— Exam 2
? 5.

mation to help consumers move through the decision-making process to select the product that meets their needs.

Promotion is the primary way that businesses communicate with prospective customers. Businesses use promotion to inform consumers about the features and benefits of their products and services and to encourage them to buy.

Effective promotion is based on effective communications. You learned about the elements of a communications model in Chapter 10. In promotion, the company that develops the promotion is the sender. The

ILLUSTRATION 23-4

How do businesses communicate with prospective customers?

information in the promotion is the message, and the method of promotion (advertising, personal selling, sales promotion) determines the communication medium. The prospective consumer is the receiver. Feedback from the receiver will help the sender determine if the promotion was successful and to adjust the message, if needed. Forms of promotion that businesses commonly use to communicate with customers are advertising, personal selling, and sales promotions, such as coupons, sampling, and in-store displays.

■ ADVERTISING

Advertising is any form of paid promotion that delivers a message to many people at the same time. Because the message is designed to appeal to many people, it will be rather impersonal. However, since the message will reach thousands of people, the cost of communicating with each person is very low.

Organizations spend more money each year in the United States on advertising than on any other type of promotion. While the average business spends less than 2 percent of total sales annually on advertising, some businesses spend over 20 percent. Companies in industries such as beverages, cosmetics, and electronics depend on advertising and spend a significant amount throughout the year to keep their brand names in front of consumers.

■ ADVERTISING PURPOSES AND MEDIA CHOICES

Advertising is a powerful tool because it can help a business accomplish a variety of objectives. Companies need to consider carefully what they want to communicate to consumers and plan specific advertising to accomplish that communication goal. The major purposes of advertising are shown in Figure 23-4.

FACTS AND FIGURES

In 1998, the U.S. corporation that spent the most dollars on advertising was General Motors, which spent almost $3 billion dollars.

FIGURE 23-4

Advertising can accomplish many purposes. Businesses carefully plan each ad to focus on a specific purpose.

1. To inform and educate consumers.
2. To introduce a new product or business.
3. To announce an improvement or product change.
4. To reinforce important product features and benefits.
5. To increase the frequency of use of a product.
6. To increase the variety of uses of a product.
7. To convince people to enter a store.
8. To develop a list of prospects.
9. To make a brand, trademark, or slogan familiar.
10. To improve the image of a company or product.
11. To gain support for ideas or causes.

PUBLICATION ADVERTISING

newspapers, general and special interest magazines, business and professional journals, and directories

MASS MEDIA ADVERTISING

radio, network and local television, cable television

OUTDOOR ADVERTISING

billboards, signs, posters, vehicle signage, and electronic displays

DIRECT ADVERTISING

sales letters, catalogs, brochures, inserts, telemarketing, fax messages, and computer databases

DISPLAY ADVERTISING

window, counter, and aisle displays; special signage; self-service merchandising; trade show displays

INTERNET ADVERTISING

static banner, interactive banner, buttons, sponsored site, cooperative site listings, e-mail list development

FIGURE 23-5

Types of Advertising Media by Categories

Most businesses use some form of advertising to attract prospective customers. However, the methods of reaching consumers—the advertising media—vary a great deal. **Advertising media** are the methods of delivering the promotional message to the intended audience. The most widely used forms of advertising media are classified by categories in Figure 23-5.

■ PLANNING AND MANAGING ADVERTISING

Businesses have many choices of media to use to communicate information to customers. However, planning an advertising program involves more than selecting the media. Advertising should be planned to support other promotion and marketing decisions. Most businesses that spend a significant amount of money for advertising throughout the year develop an advertising plan. The plan outlines the communications goals and specifies a calendar of advertising activities, an advertising budget, and how the advertising will be evaluated.

Small businesses often need help in developing their advertising plans and in writing their advertisements. A printing company may have specialists who help in writing the copy and designing the advertisement for a direct-mail piece. The people who sell advertising space may offer suggestions in preparing newspaper advertisements. Radio and television station marketing people may also help plan advertising.

As the business grows, the owner has the option of hiring someone to handle the advertising or of placing all of the company's advertising planning in the hands of an advertising agency. Full-service agencies provide all of the services related to planning and producing advertisements for all media and buying the space or time for the ads in the media. Most agencies also offer research services to determine customers' product and information needs. For their services, advertising agencies usually charge a percentage of the total amount spent for the advertising, but may charge for the actual costs of developing and placing the ads.

Some very large companies have a complete advertising department that performs all of the functions of an ad agency. Because of the amount of advertising large companies do and its cost, it is more efficient for those companies to have their own advertising personnel than to pay an ad agency.

THE ADVERTISING BUDGET Companies allot an amount for advertising when they develop their overall company budget. Most businesses plan the advertising program for one year or less. Of course, emergencies may arise that require a quick decision, but planning helps avoid budget misuse. If the company is developing a new product, it will usually prepare an advertising budget to support the new product's introduction into the market.

Large businesses often develop separate advertising budgets for new products, product lines, customer groups, or regions of a market. Separate budgets make it is easier to determine the results of specific advertising on sales and profits.

The amount a business spends on advertising depends more on the characteristics of the product and target market than on the competition. A business with a loyal group of customers and a product that has been in the market for a long time may need to spend less than a business with a new or very complex product or one that is in an extremely competitive market. A business that relies on advertising for the majority of its promotion will, of course, spend a larger percentage of sales on advertising than a business that has a balanced promotional program of advertising, personal selling, and sales promotion.

TIMING OF ADVERTISING Advertising is more effective at some times than others. Companies determine the times when potential customers are most willing and able to buy the products or services advertised. Many products and services are seasonal, with the majority of sales concentrated in a few months of the year. Companies spend more advertising dollars during those times when consumers are considering the purchase of the product than during times when customers are less likely to buy. For example, advertising for ski resorts or ocean cruises increases during the winter months, while advertising for air conditioners and lawn mowers appears most in the spring and summer.

Occasionally, companies advertise to increase purchases at times customers do not traditionally consider buying the product. By emphasizing new product development and advertising, turkey producers and processors have increased the sale of turkey products throughout the year. Those businesses had previously sold almost all of their products near the Thanksgiving holiday and one or two other holiday times during the year.

A single advertisement may produce temporary results, but regular advertising is important in building a steady stream of customers. If advertising does not appear often enough, customers tend to forget about the business or product. To keep their name and brands fresh in consumers' minds, businesses often spread their advertising over the entire year. Only when the company wants an immediate impact, such as for a new product introduction or for a special event, would it consider a large, one-time expenditure.

PERSONAL SELLING

Personal selling is promotion through direct, personal contact with a customer. The salesperson usually makes direct contact with the customer through a face-to-face meeting. There are many types of customers, and a salesperson must be able to adjust to each. Some customers know exactly what they want, while others are in the early stages of decision-making. A critical sales skill is understanding the customer's motivations.

STUDYING THE WANTS OF CUSTOMERS

Individuals are motivated to buy for different reasons. **Buying motives** are the reasons people buy. Some common consumer buying motives are listed in Figure 23-6. To be successful, the salesperson must determine a particular customer's buying motive and then tailor the sales presentation to appeal to that motive. In many cases, the salesperson can appeal to more than one buying motive. For instance, a laundry company representative, in attempting to sell laundry services to a working couple with three children, may talk about the comfort and convenience of having the laundry done outside the home rather than doing it themselves. The salesperson may also explain that

Status	**Ease of use**	**Affection**
Appetite	**Love of beauty**	**Wealth**
Comfort	**Amusement**	**Enjoyment**
Desire for bargains	**Desire for good health**	**Pride of ownership**
Recognition	**Friendship**	**Fear**

FIGURE 23-6

Understanding common buying motives of consumers is an important selling skill.

GLOBAL PERSPECTIVE

CHAIBOL—THE SOUTH KOREAN CYBER-BUYING CLUB

Combine a unique cultural buying motive, the technology of the Internet, and effective pricing and you have a rapidly growing sales tool in South Korea. In 1998, the South Korean company Samsung tried to find a way to help its 185,000 employees through a difficult economic time by developing a group purchasing program using the Internet. Employees purchasing products offered by the company on their Internet "cybermall" known as Chaibol were given a 15 percent discount on the price of the products.

A unique aspect of the South Korean culture is that there is a strong commitment to group purchasing. Employee groups, groups of professionals, and even alumni of schools encourage each other to purchase from Internet sites set up specifically for their group. In addition to providing products for sale, the cyber communities offer chat rooms, bulletin boards, group information and news, and their own personal home pages. The cyber groups reduce the amount of promotion required and also allow companies to sell products at a lower cost because of the increased volume resulting from group purchasing.

Even Samsung was surprised by the success of the Chaibol. The Internet site increased its membership to 1.2 million customers within two years and expects to add at least another million in the third year. Sales are expected to top $1 billion dollars by 2005 with net profits of $45 million dollars.

For years, South Korean society has had many social networks formed around employee groups. So, it has been much easier to extend the buying club services to those existing groups. Samsung now establishes similar Internet services for many businesses. It has formed a partnership with Freechal.com to open a site called Samsung Mall that is available to anyone. However, it still uses purchasing clubs as the primary method of signing up customers, continuing to build on the cultural need to belong to a group. The next step for Samsung is to develop an agreement with one of South Korea's largest parcel delivery services to be able to guarantee 24-hour delivery of products ordered on the Internet.

THINK CRITICALLY

1. Why do you believe Internet shopping grew so rapidly among Samsung employees in the first two years of the new cybermall business?
2. What causes Internet sales to increase when Samsung develops specialized cyber communities and includes chat rooms, information services, and home pages developed specifically for a particular group of consumers?
3. Do you think the culture of the U.S. would support the same approach to developing Internet shopping groups as was done in South Korea? Why or why not? Are there examples of successful shopping groups in the U.S. that have developed without the use of the Internet? For those you can identify, what has made them successful?

Source: *BusinessWeek Online, March 20, 2000 (http://www.businessweek.com/2000)*

it is less expensive to send the laundry to a professional service because of all the expenses involved in doing laundry at home.

Suppose that this same salesperson calls on the owner of a barber shop or beauty salon. Here the salesperson can emphasize the special sterilizing treatment given to towels, capes, and uniforms and the speed of delivering the laundered items. Both the family and the business owner might find individually scheduled pickup and delivery services attractive. Providing customer satisfaction through a sale is the ultimate goal of a salesperson. This method of selling does not require high-pressure selling; it requires intelligent customer-oriented selling.

■ PRESENTING AND DEMONSTRATING THE PRODUCT

Customers are interested in what the product will do for them and how they can use it. Salespeople must have a thorough knowledge of the product, so they can provide accurate information and answer questions. For example, customers might ask the following questions: "How much paint will I need for a bathroom 12 feet by 8 feet?" "Which vinyl is best for a concrete basement floor?" "Why is this pair of shoes $68 and that pair $55?" Different customers will value different types of information about the same product. Salespeople should study the products they sell as well as the competition's products, so they can be prepared to answer any questions customers might ask. Nothing is more frustrating than to have a salesperson talk at length about product information that is of no interest to the customer.

In addition to giving customers information, salespeople should be able to demonstrate the use of the product, so that customers can determine whether or not the product will meet their needs. It is usually a good idea for salespeople to show the product and its uses at the same time that they provide information about it. The salesperson can then focus the customer's attention on the product while explaining its features and advantages. Whenever possible, salespeople should encourage the customer to participate. When a customer is directly involved and becomes comfortable with use of the product, initial interest can change to the desire to own the product.

In certain selling situations, such as selling very large or bulky products or selling services, salespeople demonstrate without having the actual product. They use items such as photographs, charts, catalogs, videotapes, or computer displays. Such situations make it more difficult for the customer to get a true feeling for the use of a product, so the salesperson will have to rely on effective communications to increase understanding and desire to purchase the product.

■ ANSWERING CUSTOMER QUESTIONS

A customer usually has many questions during the salesperson's presentation and demonstration. The salesperson should not be concerned by the questions but should view them as an opportunity to better understand the customer's needs and help the customer make the best decision.

When customers are not certain whether the product is suitable for them, they may raise objections. **Objections** are concerns or complaints expressed by the customer. Objections may represent real concerns. However, they may simply be an effort to avoid making a decision to purchase. It is difficult to try to second-guess a customer to determine if the objection is real or not. It is best for the salesperson to listen carefully to the objection, and then help the customer make the best decision.

◼ CLOSING THE SALE

For many salespeople, the most difficult part of the selling process is asking the customer to buy. As you saw in Figure 23-3, a decision to purchase involves several steps, and each customer moves through those steps in a different way and at a different speed.

If the salesperson has involved the customer in the sales presentation and has listened carefully to the customer's needs, the customer's interest in buying should be rather apparent. Typically, effective salespeople give the customer the opportunity to buy several times during the sales presentation by asking for a decision on a specific model, color, price, or type of payment. If the customer continues to ask questions, the salesperson will answer the questions and continue the discussion until the customer appears satisfied. Then the salesperson will attempt to close the sale again.

Many sales, particularly for expensive products, take several meetings between the salesperson and the customer. In business-to-business selling, teams of salespeople and specialists from the company may meet several times with teams of buyers from the customer's company. Several people will likely make the final decision. Salespeople should continue to work with the customers until it is clear that they do not want the product or until the sale is made.

◼ FOLLOW-UP

The selling process is not complete just because the customer agrees to purchase a product. Effective marketing results in satisfying exchanges between a business and a customer. Selling is successful only when the customer is satisfied. Satisfied customers lead to repeat sales that help the company remain profitable in the future.

A plan for retaining customers includes several follow-up activities after the sale. The salesperson should check with the customer to be sure that the order is correct, the customer knows how to use the product, and that it meets the customer's needs. If there are problems, they should be corrected immediately. If following up with each customer is impractical, the business could periodically conduct a customer satisfaction survey. This could be done through an in-store, mailed, or e-mailed questionnaire or through phone calls to random customers. The follow-up contact will remind satisfied customers where they made their purchases, so they may choose to buy from the business again.

■ SALES PROMOTIONS

Sales promotions are any promotional activities other than advertising and personal selling intended to motivate customers to buy. Some sales promotions are designed to encourage customers to buy immediately. Others are designed to display the products in an attention-getting or attractive way to encourage customers to examine the products.

Coupons are a type of sales promotion used extensively to promote consumer products. Coupons are an effective method of increasing sales of a product for a short time. They are used principally to introduce a new product or to maintain and increase a company's share of the market for established brands. Coupons usually appear in newspaper and magazine advertisements, but they are also distributed by direct mail and are now even available on the Internet. A coupon packaged with a product the customer just purchased may encourage the customer to buy the same brand the next time. Or the enclosed coupon may be for another product from the same company, to encourage the customer to try it.

Manufacturers often cooperate with wholesalers and retailers by providing promotional materials. Some of these promotional materials, commonly furnished without cost or at a low price, include window displays, layouts and illustrations for newspaper ads, direct-mail inserts, display materials, and sales presentation aids.

ILLUSTRATION 23-5

How do businesses use coupons as a sales promotion tool?

CYBER COMMUNICATION

Free e-mail can be obtained over the World Wide Web at advertisement-based e-mail providers. As you can guess, advertising pays for the service. You don't need special software to use this type of e-mail; however, if you want to subscribe, you must provide personal information that is shared with advertisers on the site.

The best free e-mail systems will advertise to you by way of your e-mail account. As you visit their sites, you will see ads that you can click on or disregard. However, some free e-mail systems want you to provide your name and personal address and phone number. This information is then shared with advertisers or other users. Some systems even require a credit card number.

ACTIVITY Think about whether a free e-mail system is actually "free." Ask friends or family members if they have had experience with free e-mail. Discuss in class whether there are any rules that a person should follow when using such systems.

When producers are introducing a new product, they may distribute samples through the mail. The purpose of this activity is to familiarize people with the products to create a demand for them in local businesses. Coupons often accompany the samples to encourage the consumer to go to a local store and buy the product.

Producers and distributors also cooperate with retailers by arranging special displays and demonstrations within stores. For example, demonstrators may cook and distribute samples of a new brand of hot dog to customers in a grocery store. This practice usually helps the retailers sell the new product. The retailer, of course, gives this merchandise preference over other competing products because of this special promotion. Sometimes distributors pay merchants for the privilege of giving demonstrations or offer special prices for the opportunity.

Today, store designs, displays, labels, and packaging promote products so well that many stores let these promotions alone sell the products, rather than employ many salespeople. In **self-service merchandising,** customers select the products they want to purchase, take them to the checkout counter, and pay for them, without much help from salespeople. The display of merchandise in self-service stores attracts attention and makes it convenient for the shopper to examine the merchandise. The labels on the merchandise provide adequate information about the merchandise for the shopper to make a decision.

■ TRUTH IN ADVERTISING AND SELLING

Laws and regulations protect consumers from unfair promotional practices. Nationally, the Federal Trade Commission and the Federal Communications Commission are responsible for regulating promotion. False advertising is a violation of the law. **False advertising** is defined by federal law as "misleading in a material respect" or in any way that could influence the customer's purchase or use of the product.

To protect consumers, advertisers are required to use **full disclosure,** providing all information necessary for consumers to make an informed decision. They must also use **substantiation**—that is, be able to prove all claims they make about their products and services Exam 2 ? 12 in promotions.

If businesses violate laws and regulations in their advertising, they may face three types of penalties from the regulating agencies: (1) The agency may impose a **cease and desist order,** which requires the company to stop using specific advertisements. (2) In situations where the advertising has harmed consumers, the company may be required to spend a specified amount of its advertising budget to run corrective advertising. **Corrective advertising** is new advertising designed to change the false impression left by the misleading information. (3) In unusual situations, the company may have to pay a fine to the government or to the consumers harmed by its illegal advertising.

Long-term business success is built on honesty and fair practices. A businessperson may occasionally be tempted to exaggerate or to imitate a competitor who seems to be stretching the truth. In the long run, however, it does not pay to destroy customers' confidence. If customers do not get what they believed was promised to them in advertisements or by salespeople, they will likely not return to the business. On the other hand, a satisfied customer is often an important source of promotion for a business.

CHAPTER CONCEPTS

■ Businesses as well as consumers must make careful buying decisions. In a successful exchange, the customer is satisfied with the purchase and the company makes a reasonable profit.

■ Businesses must decide what to buy, when to buy, from whom to buy, and how much to buy. Mistakes will result in unsold products, dissatisfied customers, and losses rather than profits.

■ When setting the price to charge for a product, businesspeople consider payment terms, discounts, and the elements that make up a product's price—the cost of goods sold, operating expenses, margin, and net profit. Price strategies include pricing to meet competition, to earn a specific profit, to sell more products, or to provide customer services.

■ Businesses attempt to control costs by establishing practices that will help reduce markdowns, damaged or stolen merchandise, and the need for customers to return merchandise.

■ Even good products require effective promotion. The most common methods of promotion are advertising, personal selling, and sales promotion. Well-designed promotion follows a model for effective communications.

■ Advertising is paid promotion directed at a large number of people at the same time. While the cost of advertising is quite high, since it reaches many people, the cost of communicating with each person is usually very low. An advertising plan outlines the communication goals and specifies the timing, budget, and evaluation criteria for the advertising.

■ Personal selling is selling through direct personal contact with a customer. It requires an understanding of buying motives. Salespeople study the wants and needs of customers, demonstrate the product, answer customer questions, and close the sale when customers are prepared to make a purchase decision. The sale is complete when the salesperson follows up with the customer to determine if he or she is satisfied with the purchase.

■ The Federal Trade Commission and the Federal Communications Commission protect consumers from unfair and illegal promotion. Companies must be able to prove all claims made in ads and can be asked to stop using illegal ads, run corrective advertising, or even pay a fine. Illegal advertising usually results in dissatisfied customers who will take their business elsewhere.

BUILD VOCABULARY POWER

Define the following terms and concepts.

1. list price
2. discounts
3. trade discount
4. quantity discount
5. seasonal discount
6. cash discount

7. selling price
8. cost of good sold
9. operating expenses
10. margin (gross profit)
11. net profit
12. markup
13. markdown
14. advertising
15. advertising media
16. personal selling
17. buying motives
18. objections
19. sales promotions
20. self-service merchandising
21. false advertising
22. full disclosure
23. substantiation
24. cease and desist order
25. corrective advertising

REVIEW FACTS

1. What four specific decisions do business buyers make when they plan a purchase?
2. What two factors affect a business's choice of product assortment?
3. What are the pros and cons for a business of buying from just one or a few suppliers?
4. Once a buyer and seller have agreed on a purchase, how are the goods ordered?
5. What are some examples of terms of sale offered by suppliers? Compare and contrast your examples.
6. Why is the price of a product important to both the customer and the business?
7. What is the result if operating expenses are higher than a product's margin?
8. What components make up a product's selling price?
9. How has the Internet affected the prices businesses can charge for their products?
10. While businesses cannot totally eliminate markdowns, how can they control them?
11. Why might a company have very good products yet not be able to sell them?
12. Compare promotion to the elements of effective communication and analyze how sales promotion materials encourage sales.
13. What types of help are available to small businesses when planning advertising?
14. Why should companies spread their advertising throughout the year rather than spending most of their advertising budget at one time?
15. Why should a salesperson demonstrate a product for a customer?
16. Identify several promotional methods other than advertising and personal selling.

DISCUSS IDEAS

1. Why is it important for businesses to consider both the customer and the business when planning the sale of products?

2. Identify a product that you purchase regularly. For that product, review the four purchasing decisions that should be made by a company that wants to sell that product to you and your friends: what to purchase, when to purchase, from whom to purchase, and how much to purchase.

3. Why would a company want to offer discounts to buyers rather than selling products at the list price?

4. Using the formula for calculating net profit, suggest several ways that a business can increase the net profit from the sale of a product.

5. How can a company actually sell more products yet earn less net profit or actually lose money from the sales?

6. Explain why high-technology products are often sold initially at very high prices, but then the price begins to drop rather dramatically.

7. Some companies have a policy of accepting returned merchandise with very few questions about why the customer is returning the product. Provide reasons for and against that policy. Consider both the customer and the business in developing your answer.

8. "Promotion is the primary way that businesses communicate with prospective customers." Is communication the primary goal of promotion, or does promotion have a more important goal?

9. Which advertising media do you believe are most effective for the products you purchase? Why? Would the same media be most effective for advertising the products your parents buy? Why or why not?

10. Why do you believe that closing the sale is the most difficult step of the selling process for many salespeople? As a customer, what would you recommend to salespeople to make that step easier and more successful?

ANALYZE INFORMATION

1. A dress shop featuring prom dresses purchased 100 dresses at $125 each. The shop priced the dresses at $300 each and sold 50 dresses at that price. For the dresses not sold, the shop reduced the price to $225 and sold 30 dresses at that price. It then sold the remaining dresses for $100. What was the dollar amount of sales? What was the cost of goods sold? What was the gross profit?

2. A hobby shop has been selling an average of 10 model airplane motors each month that cost $20 each. The regular selling price has been $28. By reducing the selling price to $24, the shop increased the number of sales to 15 each month. If the average monthly operating expenses were increased a total of $10 by the change, how much was the monthly net profit increased or decreased by the change in price?

3. A book and gift store that has average annual sales of $700,000 spends 3 percent of its sales for advertising. The store's advertising budget is divided as follows: catalogs, 30 percent; calendars and other sales promotions, 7 percent; window displays, 15 percent; newspaper advertising, 15 percent; direct mail, 20 percent; and miscellaneous, 13 percent.

   a. How much is the average annual advertising budget?

   b. What is the amount spent on each type of advertising?

4. Find online examples of each of the following types of advertising: static banner, interactive banner, button, sponsored site, cooperative site listing with another Internet site, e-mail list development. Print each advertisement you find and prepare a display of the various types of Internet advertising.

5. Assume that you are a salesperson in a furniture store. Explain the buying motives you believe might be prompting each of the following types of customers to consider buying a sofa sleeper: (a) a college student who is buying furniture for a one-bedroom apartment, (b) a family that is outfitting a family room they are remodeling, and (c) a motel owner who is deciding between a less-expensive sofa and the sofa sleeper for 50 rooms.

SOLVE BUSINESS PROBLEMS

CASE 23-1

Kuen Young is planning to open a small convenience grocery store in a town of 50,000 people. Two well-known supermarket chains also serve the town. One chain is a cash-and-carry supermarket where customers must bag their own merchandise. The store offers no special services and stocks mostly private brands at relatively low costs but offers a wide variety of grocery and non-grocery items.

   The second supermarket offers a selection of several national brands for most products. Its prices are much higher than the prices of the first chain, but it offers many customer services including an on-site branch of a community bank, a place to pay utility bills, and a package wrapping and mailing service. The supermarket is considering adding a service where customers can send in orders by fax or the Internet and then pick up the order.

   Kuen's store will be located in a new housing development on the opposite end of town from the two supermarkets. At this point few homeowners live in the housing development, but it is expected to grow a great deal over the next three years. Right now, few businesses are located in the new housing areas, but that also is expected to change as more people move into the area.

Think Critically:

1. What types of grocery products and services should Kuen offer to compete with the two supermarkets?

2. What other products might Kuen carry in addition to grocery items to attract customers from the supermarkets?
3. How should Kuen decide on the prices to charge for the products he carries in his new business?
4. What effect do you think the planned growth in numbers of customers and possible new businesses will have on the decisions Kuen makes about his convenience store?
5. Develop a customer retention plan that will help Kuen build customer loyalty.

CASE 23-2

Peter and Torrie were discussing how companies use advertising:

Peter: *Companies spend too much money on advertising. If they would spend less, the prices of products would be a lot lower. I heard that companies that advertise on the Super Bowl program spend more than $1 million for one advertisement.*

Torrie: *It seems that companies advertise to get people to buy products they don't want. I've bought some things just because of the ad and regretted it later. Companies with good products shouldn't have to advertise. People will find out about them from others who try the products and like them.*

Peter: *The worst thing about advertising is that businesses can say anything they want to about products, even if the statements are untrue. They often criticize their competitors, making you think there's something wrong with the other product. After watching or listening to an ad, you're more confused than ever about what to buy.*

Think Critically:

1. Do you believe product prices would decrease if companies did not advertise? Explain.
2. Do good products need to be advertised? Why or why not?
3. What types of controls are there on what a business can say in its advertising? What can consumers do if they believe they have been misled by advertising?
4. Do you believe advertising results in more confusion than help for consumers? Justify your answer.

PROJECT: MY BUSINESS, INC.

A businessperson must set prices on products that will provide a reasonable net profit. In addition, a new business needs to plan promotion to introduce people to the business and its products and to encourage customers to try the products.

DATA COLLECTION

1. Many Internet sites offer information on start-up expenses for small businesses in general and the type of juice business you are starting specifically. Locate sources of that information and develop a list of the common types of expenses and the range of costs you might expect to begin your business.
2. Interview one or two small business owners. Ask them to explain the terms and policies of some of the vendors they deal with.
3. Interview one or two small business owners in your community. Ask them to explain the types of promotion they use, what assistance they get to help them with promotional planning, and how they estimate the amount of money they can spend on promotional activities.
4. Collect samples of advertising and promotion that local small businesses are using. Analyze their effectiveness in communicating with prospective customers. Analyze the publicity's potential impact. Prepare possible strategies for dealing with it.
5. Check with several media that offer advertising in your community (newspapers, television, radio, etc.). Obtain a price list that indicates the costs of advertising in each medium, based on the size, type, and frequency of the advertising.

ANALYSIS

1. Assume that, in an average month, your sales will include 700 small drinks, 800 large drinks, 900 supplement additions to the drinks (beyond any free supplements), and 2,000 high-energy snack bars. First, determine the price you will charge for each product, being realistic about what you believe customers are willing to pay. Then estimate your monthly expenses for each of the following items: cost of goods sold, inventory spoilage, taxes and fees, equipment expense, interest expense, supplies, repairs and maintenance, salaries, depreciation expense, insurance, advertising, and other expenses. Have several people review your estimates to determine if they are realistic. Then calculate your estimated monthly profit or loss.
2. Is your estimated monthly net profit adequate? If not, consider what changes you could make to improve it. (Don't make any price changes at this time.) Which of the possible changes are most likely to be successful? Which are least likely to be implemented?
3. Develop a purchasing plan. Assume the monthly sales given in item 1 above. List the raw materials and supplies you will need. Determine when, how much, and from whom to buy.
4. Being as creative as possible, list several ways of promoting your new business that would be (a) informative, (b) unique, and (c) affordable. Consider methods in addition to advertising.
5. Develop a three-month promotional plan for your new business. Include methods, media to be used, time schedule, budget, and samples of the promotions.

UNIT SEVEN

HUMAN RESOURCES MANAGEMENT

CHAPTERS

People make change happen. Today's successful companies have recognized that only by investing in their most important assets –their people–can a true company transformation become a reality. People, using their knowledge and skills, are the only effective change agents for any company.

Daniel R. Tobin
Transformational Learning, 1996

HUMAN RESOURCES PLANNING

OBJECTIVES

24-1 Describe the types of activities that occur in a human resources department.

24-2 Outline the procedures to follow in identifying and selecting new personnel.

24-3 Identify factors to consider when employees are promoted, transferred, or released.

24-4 Compare three major systems that businesses use to pay employees.

24-5 Describe several common employee benefits.

24-6 Discuss how human resources management is changing in businesses today.

A HARD DECISION TO MAKE

atrick Gomez was discussing job alternatives with his parents. He had two offers and was considering which would be the best choice. Both jobs were in marketing research, the area of business in which he wanted to work. One job was for a contract research organization, which accepted research projects from many other companies. The second job was in the marketing department of an international manufacturer, where all of Patrick's projects would be for that company. He thought he would enjoy the work he would do for either of the companies.

The major difference between the job offers concerned the rate of pay and benefits offered. In the first job, Patrick would be considered a contract employee. He would receive a rate of pay of $15 per hour. He would work a minimum of 35 hours per week and most weeks would work a full 40 hours. However, there were no benefits, such as insurance and paid holidays. Patrick could take time off between projects but would receive no pay for those days. He would personally need to pay for any insurance if he wanted coverage.

The second job paid a beginning salary of $21,000 per year. Patrick would work a minimum of 40 hours per week with occasional weekend work during particularly busy times. He would receive two full weeks of paid vacation plus five additional paid holidays. The company would contribute $150 per month and Patrick would pay $35 per month for a health insurance policy providing full health and dental care. He would also have a company-paid life insurance policy worth twice the amount of his annual salary. Each year the company would contribute an amount equal to 5 percent of Patrick's salary to a retirement plan. If Patrick stayed with the company for 5 years, he would become part of the retirement plan and would be entitled to the money upon retirement. If he left before that time, the money would go back to the company.

As Patrick considered the choices, he was impressed with the possibility of earning over $31,000 per year at the first company if he worked 40 hours per week for the entire year. He had a number of school loans to pay off, and the extra money would come in handy.

However, his parents reminded him that he was not guaranteed all of those hours and would not have any vacations if he expected to earn that much money. While he had not had any major health problems, any illness could be expensive and would be covered by the health insurance of the second company but not by the first. And, even though Patrick was only 22 years old, beginning to save for retirement at an early age was an important consideration. Patrick knew he had a difficult decision to make. He had never considered how salary and benefits could affect a job decision.

Of all the resources used by a business, probably the most important to its success is people. People are responsible for the effective use of all other resources in the business. People make decisions, operate equipment, maintain records, and deal with customers. Because of their value to the business, managing people is a critical function.

All managers work with people. However, **human resources management (HRM)** consists of all activities involved with acquiring, developing, and compensating the people who do the company's work. HRM is sometimes called *personnel management*. Employees' pay, training, benefits, work environment, and many other factors contribute to their productivity, performance quality, and willingness to stay with the company. The people who work in human resources management perform the tasks that help the business keep the skilled, productive, and satisfied employees it needs to succeed.

HUMAN RESOURCES ACTIVITIES

To begin human resources planning, companies must determine the number of people they will need in order to complete all of the tasks and the skills those people will need. Then they must recruit, hire, and train those employees. Once on the job, the employees will need the equipment and other resources to accomplish their jobs. Directions provided through descriptions of job duties, policies, and procedures help the organization operate effectively. Human resources employees take part in all of these activities.

Businesses must be sure that employees are satisfied with their jobs and motivated to perform well. They need to be concerned about employee safety and health, working conditions, wages, and benefits. Employees who are doing a good job need to be recognized and rewarded, while those who are not need to be given training and support to improve their performance. In some cases employees will need to be removed from their jobs if performance does not improve or if there are major changes in company operations. As you can see, working with people involves many responsibilities.

Most companies have a department that is responsible for human resources management. Large companies may have several specialized divisions within the department, each of which deals with a specific area in human resources. Some of the human resources activities may be performed in other departments across the organization but are planned and coordinated through the human resources (HR) department. Most managers regularly use the services of the HR department as they work with their employees. Employees also receive a variety of services from the people who work in human resources. The important HR services common to many businesses are illustrated in Figure 24-1 and are described next.

EMPLOYMENT

Employment is the one area most people associate with human resources management. The employment function of human resources involves all activities required to maintain an adequate number of qualified employees for the company. Employment activities include determining the need to hire employees, recruiting applicants, determining the qualifications of applicants, and hiring the most qualified to fill the available jobs. In addition, transfers, promotions, retirements, dismissals, and other job changes are part of the employment function.

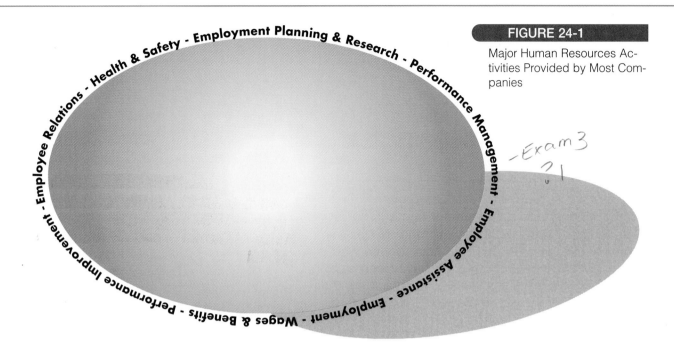

FIGURE 24-1

Major Human Resources Activities Provided by Most Companies

Exam 3 ?

ILLUSTRATION 24-1

What are some of the activities involved in the employment function of human resources management?

■ WAGES AND BENEFITS

The amount a company pays employees directly and spends to provide employee benefits such as insurance and vacation time is a major part of its operating budget. The level of wages and benefits, especially when compared to competitors, helps to determine who will

CAREER CONNECTION

HUMAN RESOURCES SPECIALIST

Human resources specialists provide a link between top management and employees. They recruit and interview employees, and advise on hiring decisions in accordance with policies and requirements that have been established with top management. They also help their firms effectively use employees' skills, provide training opportunities to enhance those skills, and boost employee satisfaction with their jobs and working conditions.

Human resources specialists are employed in virtually every industry. Some are self-employed and work as consultants to public and private employers. The private sector accounts for about 80 percent of salaried jobs.

Employers usually seek college graduates. Many employers prefer applicants who have majored in human resources, personnel administration, or industrial and labor relations. Others look for graduates with a technical or business background.

For more career information about human resources specialists, check your library or the Internet for resources.

apply for job openings and whether they are likely to make a long-term commitment to the company or will be looking for higher-paying jobs. When performing the wages-and-benefits function, HR employees plan and manage the financial and non-financial rewards available to employees.

Wages and benefits must be carefully controlled. Employee productivity (the amount of work accomplished) compared to the pay and benefits will determine whether the company can be profitable or not. It is important that employees view the system for determining pay as fair and that there is a reasonable relationship between the amount paid to an employee and the value of that employee's work to the company. Human resources is typically responsible for developing a pay system that classifies jobs according to levels and pay ranges. When a person is hired, promoted, or given a pay increase, human resources completes or monitors the procedures to ensure that the employee gets paid the correct amount.

Companies offer benefits to their employees in addition to wages. Some benefits, such as social security and Medicare, are required by law. Others, such as insurance and vacations, are not legally required, but many companies provide them. Often benefit plans are different for full-time than for part-time employees or are based on the length of time the employee has worked for the company. People who work in HR study what benefits can be offered, determine the cost of each benefit, and help management develop the benefits plan. They also provide information to employees about each type of benefit and make sure that employees recognize the value of the benefits to them.

Some companies offer employees choices of benefits, so helping employees make the best decisions and keeping track of each person's choices can be quite complicated. Once employees make their decisions, HR employees complete the necessary paperwork or enter the data into the company's computer system. Each benefit program must be monitored to control costs and to make sure employees receive the benefits to which they are entitled.

PERFORMANCE IMPROVEMENT

Companies cannot thrive with employees whose skills are the same today as they were the day they were hired. Employees must improve their skills and learn new ones on the job. The role of human resources in performance improvement involves training and educating employees to ensure high quality and efficient work. Often the HR department plans and manages performance improvement programs in cooperation with managers and individual employees.

Most businesses conduct several types of training and education programs. Once hired, employees receive an orientation to the company and initial training to make sure they are successful in the new job. Then, as equipment or procedures change, the company must prepare employees for those changes. Finally, when evaluations indicate that an employee is not performing as well as expected, the company will provide support for the employee to improve his or her performance, so that the employee's performance does not result in poor-quality products or customer service.

Employees may be promoted or transferred to a new job in the company. Part of the process of preparing employees for possible promotions or to be able to use existing employees in new jobs is a continuing education and training program. Many companies also allow employees to participate in education programs for their own personal development, believing that such programs increase employee motivation and productivity. Companies sometimes reimburse employees for some or all of the costs of the education as an employee benefit.

Finally, if the company cuts back on the number of employees, eliminates a department, or has a major change in its business activities, it may help the discharged employees prepare for new jobs. Some of those jobs may be in other parts of the company that are adding employees, but the education and training may be for jobs in other companies. It may seem strange that companies would spend money to educate employees to work for other companies. However, progressive employers view these programs as a responsibility to employees who have contributed to the company's past success. They also believe that people are more likely to work for a company that demonstrates this level of commitment to its employees.

EMPLOYEE RELATIONS

Human resources plays a major role in employee relations by ensuring effective communication and cooperation between management and employees. If a labor union is organized within a company, a very formal set of relationships exists between employees and management. The HR workers responsible for employee relations assist in negotiating the labor contract with the union and deal with employee activities and problems that relate to the contract. If employees are not represented by a union, HR still performs the same types of activities, but usually in a less formal way.

The flattened organizations of today mean fewer managers. Businesses expect employees to take more responsibility for their own work. Work teams made up of employees and managers are taking responsibility for many decisions once made just by managers. These decisions include hiring, determining how work will be performed, and improving work procedures. Human resources personnel help to prepare people for their new responsibilities and develop supporting materials, training, and computerized forms and procedures to help the teams successfully complete their new work responsibilities.

Another important area of employee relations is to assure that the company complies with all equal employment and affirmative action laws, such as the Americans with Disabilities Act (ADA). In addition, HR personnel work with employees and managers to prepare people for future job openings and promotions, as well as help them work cooperatively with each other despite individual differences. Companies are most successful when all employees have access to any job for which they are qualified and that discrimination is not a part of employment decisions or the daily work environment.

■ HEALTH AND SAFETY

Illnesses and injuries among employees are expensive for companies. If employees are unhealthy or injured, they may not be able to work. Other employees will have to complete that work, or the company must hire temporary employees to do it. Also, the cost of insurance and health care will increase when the number of employee illnesses and injuries go up. Expensive insurance is harmful to both the employee and the company.

Substance abuse can greatly increase injuries on the job. Workers under the influence of illegal drugs or alcohol have reduced dexterity and impaired judgment. As a result, they may ignore safety procedures or be unable to perform them properly. Substance abuse will also lower worker productivity and increase absenteeism.

The HR department is responsible for maintaining safe work areas and work procedures, enforcing laws and regulations related to safety and health, and providing adequate education and training in health and safety.

Most HR departments provide regular safety training, place safety posters and materials in the work place to remind workers to follow safety procedures, and monitor procedures to identify and correct possible safety problems. They also collect and report data on work-related injuries and illnesses to be sure the company and employees are well informed about the level of safety in the company and each department. Companies often reward work units that operate for a specific amount of time without a job-related injury.

Companies sometimes promote good health by maintaining a smoke-free environment and offering help for employees to stop smoking through education programs, support groups, and even financial bonuses if they quit smoking. To reduce employee absences and to cut insurance costs, many companies organize wellness and fitness programs, build and staff fitness centers, and pay for employees to enroll in health education classes.

■ PERFORMANCE MANAGEMENT

Managers regularly evaluate their employees' performance to determine how well it is meeting expectations. They identify their employees' strengths and reward them for superior performance. If they discover performance problems, they must help their employees improve and provide training, if needed.

Individual managers are responsible for evaluating the employees they supervise and using the results of the evaluation to improve performance. The role of human resources in performance management is to develop the evaluation system and materials and to educate managers and employees on the proper methods for evaluating and improving performance. Human resources personnel work with managers and experienced employees to design the performance management system and then prepare the forms and materials needed. They then train the managers to be able to evaluate employees objectively, complete the evaluation forms, and conduct evaluation conferences with the employees. They also help employees understand their role in the evaluation process. The HR department usually maintains the results of the evaluations in each employee's personnel file.

A newer method of performance evaluation, **360-degree feedback,** uses performance feedback gathered from a broad range of people with whom the employee works, both inside and outside the organization—rather than from just the employee's manager. People who are peers of the employee contribute performance feedback. For example, a manager gathers feedback from other managers who work at the same level; employees receive feedback from co-workers. In addition, the 360-degree feedback system includes information from people who report to the person being reviewed. Sometimes even suppliers and customers are asked for feedback.

In the 360-degree feedback system, people completing the reviews fill out a detailed questionnaire about the person's performance. The responses are anonymous, so the person evaluated does not know who specifically provided the information. Finally, the information is summarized, a report is prepared, and a performance improvement conference is held with an evaluation expert to ensure that the employee and manager interpret the information correctly and know how to use it to improve future performance.

■ EMPLOYEE ASSISTANCE PROGRAMS

Today, businesses recognize that employees have many important responsibilities in addition to their jobs. Personal and family concerns may interfere with an employee's work. Issues ranging from financial problems to marriage and family issues and alcohol or drug abuse are increasingly common among employees. **Employee assistance programs** provide confidential personal problem-solving, counseling, and support services for employees. For the most part, participating in the services is voluntary, and employees can choose to receive assistance whenever they need the help and support. For serious problems that are interfering with work, managers can refer employees to specific assistance services but, again, the employee can choose not to accept the assistance. For these types of employee assistance programs, the company hires specialists such as counselors, psychologists, and medical personnel to provide the services.

Some employee assistance programs have expanded to provide services needed by single-parent or two-working-parent families, employees in transition because of job changes or moving to a new location, and even special financial services such as short-term loans or financial assistance for education. HR personnel involved in employee assistance programs may arrange day-care services for children or elderly parents, help with short-term housing needs, plan for car pooling or other transportation services, and facilitate many other activities that help employees balance work and personal lives.

■ EMPLOYMENT PLANNING AND RESEARCH

You can see from the HR services described above that maintaining an effective workforce is very complex. Companies change rapidly, but it may take weeks and months to hire new people, design training programs, or complete performance reviews. Federal and state employment laws as well as company policies and procedures require a great deal of information about each employee to be collected and maintained.

A major HR function involves researching and maintaining the information that managers need in order to determine personnel needs and manage the workforce. The people working in this area of human resources gather information, use computer programs to analyze that information, and maintain and review employee records as well as company and competitive employment information. They then distribute this information to managers to alert them to problems, the need for changes, and ways to improve employee productivity.

■ SELECTING PERSONNEL

Hiring new employees is one of the most expensive but important company activities. Effective selection means hiring people with the right skills for each job. Hiring people who do not meet specific job qualifi-

FACTS AND FIGURES

The Small Business Administration reports that for every $1 an employer invests in personnel screening, the employer saves $5–$16 in reduced absenteeism, productivity, turnover, safety, insurance, and in employer liability.

cations results in high training costs, dissatisfied employees, and poor performance. This section discusses some essential procedures for selecting personnel in a medium-to-large company.

■ ESTABLISHING A NEED

As a first step in the process of hiring a new employee, managers must establish that they actually need a new employee. Normally, the need develops to replace a current employee who has left the company, been promoted, or retired. If

ILLUSTRATION 24-2

Why is it important to hire employees with the right skills for each job?

the company or department is growing, new employees will be needed to complete the extra work. Changes in the operations of a department or the use of new procedures or equipment may require that new employees be hired to perform those duties.

After identifying a need, the department manager typically will work with HR to complete the hiring process. The HR department must have detailed and accurate information about the position in order to screen applicants and choose only the most qualified people to interview. To compile the needed information, companies prepare a job description and job specification for each position in the company. A **job description** is a list of the basic tasks that make up a job. A **job specification** is a list of the qualifications a worker needs to do that job.

HR employees work with managers and employees who are currently doing each job to prepare job descriptions and specifications. This information is kept on file in the HR department and is updated regularly as job requirements and activities change. The data are used in a variety of ways, but in the selection process, the information is used to recruit a pool of qualified applicants and to help determine the best candidate for the job.

■ RECRUITING APPLICANTS

After the HR department has received a request to fill a position and reviewed the job description and specifications, it needs to identify applicants for the opening. An effective recruitment process will result in a number of applicants from which a well-qualified person can be selected. If the pool of qualified applicants is too small, the chances of finding someone who is well-qualified decreases. If the pool is too large, the process of selecting the most-qualified will take longer.

Many sources of prospective employees exist. The HR department must be aware of those sources and use those most likely to locate qualified applicants. Some of the most often-used sources of prospective employees are discussed next.

CURRENT EMPLOYEES Normally companies make information about all job vacancies available to everyone in the company and give current employees the first opportunity to apply. There are many reasons for using this source. The job may be a promotion for some employees, which can serve as an incentive to work harder. If it is not a promotion, allowing an employee to change jobs may provide better work hours or pay. The new job may match the employee's interests and abilities better. Placing a current employee in a job opening is also good practice for companies that are anticipating employment cutbacks.

Current employees may also recommend people they know for open positions in the company. Employees will need specific information about job openings and the procedures they should use to nominate people for openings. They must also know that the people recommended will be treated fairly and in the same way as other job applicants.

UNSOLICITED APPLICATIONS A business that has a reputation as a good employer is likely to have people applying for jobs at all times. Most large companies take applications regularly, even when they currently have no openings that fit the applicants. As applications arrive, human resources screens them for minimum qualifications and classifies them according to job categories in the company. Then they maintain the applications in an active file for a period of time, such as six months, and review them when openings occur.

EMPLOYMENT AGENCIES Employment agencies are businesses that actively recruit, evaluate, and help people prepare for and locate jobs. All states maintain an employment service supported by state and federal taxes. Public employment offices are usually located in several cities throughout each state. They offer testing services, job listings, and help in preparing applications and in developing interviewing skills. They will work with businesses to publicize available jobs and to identify qualified candidates for job openings.

OTHER SOURCES Colleges and universities, vocational and technical schools, and an increasing number of high schools have placement offices to assist graduates in obtaining jobs. Businesses can use those offices to obtain lists of potential employees and, in some cases, to obtain resumes and other information about the school's graduates.

The offices may provide assistance in scheduling interviews with a number of applicants to help the recruiting business.

Advertising is a common method of obtaining job applicants. Companies frequently advertise when they need a large number of employees or they must fill an opening quickly. HR employees carefully write employment advertisements to attract only qualified applicants, rather than large numbers of unqualified people.

The Internet has become a popular resource for recruiting personnel. Web sites such as monster.com provide thousands of job listings that job seekers can search by category of job, location, company, or salary expectations. Many employment sites on the Web also provide places where people seeking employment can post their resumes. Some sites provide services, such as help in resume preparation. Most major Internet employment sites make it possible for applicants to submit their resumes to prospective employers online. Today, companies that regularly hire employees place a link to employment opportunities on their home page, so that prospective employees can obtain an up-to-date listing of available jobs.

■ PROCESSING APPLICATIONS

Most job seekers fill out an application form, which must ask only for information necessary to make the best selection for the job. The form must not ask for discriminatory or illegal data. Then, this process is used to make the final selection:

1. HR employees review the applications to eliminate the people who do not meet minimum qualifications. Those qualifications would typically include level of education, specific training, certifications, or licenses. Applicants are often eliminated at this stage because they filled out the application form incorrectly, did not fully complete the application, or had very poor written communication skills.

2. An HR employee interviews the remaining applicants to confirm information on the application, to gather information on oral communications and human relations skills, and to provide more information to the applicants about the company and the job.

3. An HR employee checks the information supplied on the application form and through the interview for accuracy by contacting schools attended, previous employers, and listed references. Careful questioning of a reference can often reveal important information about an applicant's strengths, work habits, and human relations skills.

4. HR employees administer tests to the applicants remaining in the pool at this point to determine if the applicants have the needed knowledge and skills for the specific job. To be legal, the tests must measure only characteristics important for success on the job.

5. The manager or a work team of the department that has the opening then interviews the top applicants. The interview allows more

FACTS AND FIGURES

Employees regularly leave their companies for new jobs or even new careers, only to return when things don't work out. And employers, desperate for qualified employees and disenchanted with expensive candidate searches, are taking them back. They are called "boomerang" employees, and they compose as much as a third of the U.S. work force.

— Exam 3
? 11.

specific questioning related to the duties and qualifications for the job, can offer applicants detailed information about the job and the department, and give applicants the opportunity to ask questions. By understanding the job and its requirements, applicants will be in a better position to determine if the job would satisfy them.

6. The final selection is made by comparing information gathered with the job requirements. The decision should be made carefully and objectively to select the best applicant for the job. Many businesses require prospective employees to pass a physical exam, including drug screening. They also check for a possible criminal record. Although drug screening and background checks can help businesses avoid hiring people who might become problem employees, these checks can be considered an invasion of privacy.

7. When an applicant is hired, HR employees walk the new employee through filling out the necessary paperwork, such as tax forms and insurance enrollment forms. They then help the new employee get a good start by offering an orientation program and initial training. After the new employee has been at work for several weeks, the HR department may follow up to see whether the right person was selected, in order to improve employment procedures.

Assigning a buddy or mentor to a new employee can be extremely valuable. This person can educate the employee about whom to contact concerning different problems. The mentor can act as a resource if the new employee has questions or experiences difficulties in the first month or two on the job.

PROMOTING, TRANSFERRING, AND RELEASING EMPLOYEES

The amount of time and money invested in recruiting, hiring, and training a new employee is very high. Because of the expense, once the company finds a good employee, it should attempt to keep that person as long as possible. Offering employees opportunities for promotions and transfers can help retain good employees. The company also needs a procedure for dealing with employees who are not performing satisfactorily and for reducing the number of employees if changing economic conditions require downsizing.

A **promotion** is the advancement of an employee within a company to a position with more authority and responsibility. Usually, a promotion includes an increase in pay and may include greater prestige and benefits. Promotion opportunities occur when another person vacates a job (through promotion or retirement, for example) or when the company creates a new position.

Whenever possible, a business should fill vacancies by promotion. If the company has an effective selection procedure, it should have well-qualified employees who, with training and experience, could be promoted. Every employee should have an equal opportunity to receive promotions for which they are qualified. Employees need to know the job to which they can advance and the factors considered in promotion. Many companies now provide career counseling services for employees. Through career counseling, employees can plan career paths, determine the education and training required for the jobs in the career path, and develop plans to prepare for the jobs they want. You will learn more about employee development in the next chapter.

A **transfer** is the assignment of an employee to another job in the company that, in general, involves the same level of responsibility and authority as the person's current work. There are many reasons for transfers:

1. Employees being trained for management positions may be transferred among several positions to gain experience.
2. Employees may be transferred to give them a better opportunity for promotion.
3. Employees may be transferred to new departments or new company locations due to growth or reduction of the size of departments.
4. Employees may choose to transfer to jobs that better meet their current interests and needs.
5. Employees may be transferred to overcome difficulties resulting from poor performance or conflicts with other people on the job.

Some situations require employees to leave the company. Some employee separations are permanent, while others are temporary. They may result from a downturn in the economy or in the company's fortunes. Employees may also be released due to violations of company policies or continuing unsatisfactory job performance with no success in improving the performance.

A **discharge** is the release of an employee from the company due to inappropriate work behavior. In ordinary language, this means that the employee is fired. A **layoff** is a temporary or permanent reduction in the number of employees because of a change in business conditions. After a layoff, employees may be called back to work when jobs become available. When a company plans a large number of layoffs, the human resources department may be asked to help the employees plan for the layoff. The HR department may help in locating other jobs, offer personal and career counseling, or provide retraining for other jobs within the company.

■ EMPLOYEE TURNOVER

Employee turnover is the rate at which people enter and leave employment in a business during a year. The rate of turnover is important to a business because the loss of experienced employees means that new employees have to be hired and trained. New employees will not be as productive as experienced ones for some time. Between the time when an experienced employee leaves and a new employee is hired, the remaining employees will often be called on to get the work done. Most companies watch their employee turnover rate carefully and make every effort to keep it low. Two common formulas for computing the rate of employee turnover are shown in Figure 24-2.

FIGURE 24-2

Methods of Calculating the
Rate of Employee Turnover

1. **Number of employees who have terminated employment with the business ÷ Average number of employees = % of employee turnover**

2. **Number of employees hired to replace employees who have terminated employment with the business ÷ Average number of employees = % of employee turnover**

An example will illustrate the difference between the two methods. Suppose that during last year 150 employees left their jobs in a company. The company hired 120 new employees to replace those who had left. The average number of employees during the year was 1,000. According to the first formula, the employee turnover was 15 percent (150/1,000). According to the second formula, it was 12 percent (120/1,000). To make it easier to study employee turnover trends, the company should use the same formula from year to year.

EXIT INTERVIEWS

Whenever an employee leaves the company, interviewing the person can gain some important feedback. An **exit interview** is a formal interview with an employee who is leaving the company to determine the person's attitudes about the company and suggestions for improvement. The exit interview provides an opportunity to learn about the causes of employee turnover and feedback about the company's policies and procedures, management, and operations. The interview procedure should be carefully planned to get important information in a way that is comfortable for the person being interviewed and to accurately record the information so it can be used to improve operations and employment procedures.

PAYING EMPLOYEES

While it is usually not the most important, one of the reasons people work is to earn money. But money is just one valuable benefit that employees receive for their labor. Other benefits include such things as paid vacations, company-sponsored health insurance, and employee assistance programs. The pay and other benefits employees receive in exchange for their labor are called **compensation.**

The method used to determine pay can be an important factor in attracting employees to the company, motivating them to give their best efforts, and retaining good employees. Therefore, the compensation system needs to offer a fair way to pay employees that encourages them to work for the company, while using the company's resources efficiently.

Many factors affect the amount of pay an employee receives. These include the skill required for the job, the work conditions, the amount of education and experience the person has, the supply and demand of that type of worker, and economic conditions.

■ WAGE AND SALARY PLANS

A **wage** is pay based on an hourly rate. **Salary** is pay based on a time-frame other than hourly, such as weekly or monthly. Salaries are most often paid to executives, supervisors, professionals, and others who do not have a fixed number of hours to work each week.

Because businesses vary a great deal in the types of work and the qualifications of employees, many methods are used to determine how employees are paid. Under some plans, employees with the same qualifications and experience are paid the same no matter what job they do or whether one is more productive than another. Other systems determine pay levels by the type of work, the amount produced, or the quality of the work.

TIME PLANS The most common payment method is to pay a certain amount for a specified period of time worked. Wages are a time-based plan. For example, an employee might earn $8.50 per hour. A salary is also based on time worked. For example, a company may pay an employee a salary of $2,800 per month, while another company may set an employee's salary at $43,800 per year. In either case, the employee will receive a regular paycheck, often on a semi-weekly or monthly basis.

Time plans are easy to administer, because pay is based directly on the amount of time worked. However, time plans do not reward employees financially who provide extra effort or do outstanding work.

ILLUSTRATION 24-3

What is the difference between a wage and a salary?

PERFORMANCE PLANS   Two types of plans pay employees for the amount of work. A **commission plan** pays employees a percentage of the volume of sales for which they are responsible. For example, a salesperson may earn a commission of 5 percent on total sales. If the salesperson makes sales worth $10,000 during one week, the salesperson would earn $500 that week. The commission system provides a direct incentive to employees because their efforts directly determine their pay. Also, the business can control costs, because pay relates directly to the amount of sales. A negative result of the commission plan is that the salesperson will concentrate on activities that lead to the largest commissions. A salesperson may try to sell products a customer doesn't need, may concentrate on larger customers while ignoring smaller but important customers, and may not complete work that seems to detract from selling time.

A similar type of performance-pay system is the piece-rate plan. The **piece-rate plan** pays the employee a fixed rate for each unit produced. An individual employee's pay in this case is based directly on the amount of work the employee produces. For example, if an employee earns 30 cents for each unit and produces 250 units in a day, the employee will earn $75 for the day.

Although piece-rate plans were first used in factories to encourage employees to increase production, companies also pay other types of employees on the basis of units of work completed. They may pay billing clerks based on the number of invoices processed, data-entry personnel according to the number of lines of copy entered, order pickers based on the number of items they pull from inventory to fill orders, and market researchers based on the number of phone interviews completed.

Well-designed pay plans based on productivity usually result in increased performance, at least in the short run. However, performance plans can make it difficult for new employees to earn a reasonable amount, since they are inexperienced and can't work as efficiently as experienced workers. Performance plans may also encourage experienced employees to find shortcuts to increase their production, resulting in quality or safety problems.

Some companies are developing innovative ways to compensate performance on specific, short-term projects that motivate employees while not adding greatly to the organization's costs. The reward is often in the form of a product or service the employee values rather than a direct wage or salary payment. Under one such plan, managers reward employees who have performed well or have accomplished a specific, challenging goal. When an individual or work team achieves the established goal, the manager provides rewards such as tickets for an upcoming athletic event or concert, gift certificates for employees to take their family out for a night on the town, or some other reward that is meaningful to the employees in recognition of their efforts.

COMBINATION PLANS To get the advantages of various types of pay systems, some companies use combination plans. A **combination plan** is a pay plan that provides each employee a small wage or salary and adds incentive pay based on the person's performance. Such a plan assures the employee a specified amount of money but allows the person to earn an additional amount based on effort. It is particularly effective for jobs that require a number of activities that do not directly result in increased production or sales. Some companies provide the incentive based on the performance of a work team or group rather than on the individual's performance, in order to encourage cooperation and group effort.

A variation of the combination plan is the use of a bonus. A **bonus** is money paid at the end of a specific but long period of time (3, 6, or 12 months) for performance that exceeds the expected standard for that time. Bonuses relate employee rewards to organizational performance, so if the work unit or company does well, employees share in the profits.

■ FACTORS AFFECTING PAY LEVELS

Determining the amount of wages and salaries is an important business decision. In addition to the type of pay plan, companies consider other factors when determining wages and salaries. For example, employees who bring more skills to the job may be more valuable to the company and therefore receive greater pay than other employees in the same job. Also, some jobs may be more important to the company than others, justifying greater pay. The company may pay more for greater experience or more years worked for the company. The supply and demand of that type of labor, current economic conditions, and the prevailing wage rates in the community and in the industry also affect the rate of pay. Companies may choose to provide especially full employee benefits rather than pay high wages. Finally, federal and state labor laws, such as laws that set minimum wages, affect employee pay.

Usually HR departments of large companies employ economists and other specialists to develop pay plans and to help determine the total amount of money that should be spent on employee compensation, including benefits. Smaller companies usually attempt to compare the wages and salaries they offer to those offered by competitors so as not to lose valuable employees to other companies as a result of low wages.

■ EMPLOYEE BENEFITS

In addition to pay, employees often receive other valuable benefits from their employer as part of their total compensation. You will recall from the scenario at the beginning of the chapter that Patrick was deciding between two jobs. One of the factors he was considering was the amount of compensation. The first job appeared to pay significantly more than the second. However, the second job provided Patrick with benefits beyond the amount of money he would earn, including paid vacations and insurance. **Employee benefits** are all forms of compensation and services the company provides to employees in addition to salaries and wages.

Employee benefits can significantly increase the total compensation an employee receives. Many companies contribute between 20 and 40 percent of an employee's wages or salary to pay for benefits. Assume that a company employed 300 people at an average salary of $30,000. In addition to the $9,000,000 to pay the salaries, the company's cost of benefits may be as much as $3,600,000.

■ CUSTOMARY BENEFITS

Many businesses make it possible for their employees to obtain insurance at lower costs through group insurance policies. Life, health, dental, and disability insurance are common types of coverage provided. In many cases, the company pays part or all of the employee's insurance premium.

Some companies offer a **profit-sharing plan,** a benefit plan that pays employees a small percentage of the company's profits at the end of the year. Profit sharing encourages employees to do things that increase company profits in order to obtain the benefit.

As employees get older and begin to consider retirement, they become increasingly concerned about the income they will have once they stop working. Retirement plans are designed to meet that need. A **pension plan** is a company-sponsored retirement plan that makes regular payments to employees after retirement. Companies with a pension plan put a percentage of employees' salaries into a pension fund. The funds are invested and earnings are used to make pension payments to retired employees. In a few pension plans, the employer pays the entire cost of the pension, but in most plans the employee makes a contribution as well or pays the entire cost of the pension contribution. Figure 24-3 summarizes the differences among common types of retirement plans.

After employees have worked for a company for a specified time, often one year, they may begin to earn vacation days. Most companies pay the employees' regular salary during vacations. In addition to earned vacations, some companies are closed for holidays and may pay their employees for those days. Other common benefits are paid or unpaid absences for personal illness, the illness or death of family members, and the birth or adoption of a child.

■ HOURS OF WORK

To respond to the changing lifestyles of workers and the operating needs of businesses, some companies have experimented with changes in the standard 40-hour, five-day workweek. One such change involves

TYPE OF PENSION	DESCRIPTION
Pension Plan	A retirement plan in which the company invests a specific amount of money for each employee, based on his or her pay, and uses the earnings to make regular payments to retirees. The company owns and manages the investments.
401k Plan	A company-sponsored retirement plan in which employees may choose to have a percentage of their pay contributed to one of several alternative investment plans selected by the employer. Investment companies, rather than the employer, manage the investments, but employees own their accounts.
IRA Plan	A retirement plan that is not company-sponsored in which employees contribute a percentage of their pay, up to a specified legal limit, in any investment plan of their choice. The employer is not involved in selecting or controlling the employees' investments. The law allows only people who are not covered by an employer's retirement plan to have an IRA.
Keogh Plan	A retirement plan designed for self-employed people, who may contribute an amount of their earnings into an investment fund managed by an investment company. Keogh plans are open to people involved in sole proprietorships or partnerships.

FIGURE 24-3

Common Types of Retirement Plans

scheduling employees to work ten hours a day for four days per week. Another variation, **flextime,** lets employees choose their own work hours, within specified limits. **Job sharing** allows two people to share one full-time job. Each person works half the time, either half days or alternate days of the week.

Companies may also stagger the workweek by having some employees start their week on days other than Monday. In this way, the business can operate seven days a week without having employees work more than five days, thereby obtaining maximum use of facilities and equipment while controlling labor costs. It is also a way to reduce traffic congestion or demands on employee services, such as parking and food services, at a specific time.

■ OTHER BENEFITS

The benefits described above are most common and are available to employees in many companies. Increasingly, businesses are providing other types of benefits for employees. Many companies provide free or low-cost parking, food services and cafeterias, and discounts on the purchase of products produced or sold by the company. Many businesses contribute to the cost of college classes or other educational programs completed by employees. More and more companies are providing parents time off to visit their children's schools. Some companies

ILLUSTRATION 24-4

Why might a company provide a benefit such as exercise classes to employees?

today even offer unique services, such as hiring someone to do gift shopping or take clothing to a dry cleaner for busy employees and offering transportation for people who carpool but need to go home due to an emergency.

Some companies offer free or low-cost professional services to employees, including financial and investment advice, lawyers, accountants, and counselors. An increasingly important benefit for employees with young children is the availability of day-care facilities. That same benefit is being extended to families with elderly parents living with them. The company may offer elder-care programs as a benefit.

As you can see, the range of employee benefits is quite broad. Companies offer new benefits as employee needs change and as companies compete to attract and keep good employees. Since individual needs can be quite different, businesses have a difficult time providing the right set of benefits for each employee. Some companies have attempted to solve that problem by letting employees choose from among a number of available benefits. A program in which employees can select the benefits that meet their personal needs is known as a **cafeteria plan.** In this program, each employee can choose among benefits with equal value or give up certain benefits and receive their cost as additional compensation.

■ THE INCREASING VALUE OF HUMAN RESOURCES

Human resources management is very important in all types of businesses. Managers faced with improving the effectiveness and profitability of their business are increasingly looking at the ways that they can improve employee performance. As employees' needs continue to change and as the cost of providing employee services and benefits increases, all managers will have to emphasize building and maintaining effective employee relations. Several areas are of special concern to companies that value their employees. Those include legal responsibilities identified through employment laws, ensuring equal opportunity for all employees, and making changes to improve the way they provide and manage HR services.

■ EMPLOYMENT LAWS

State and federal governments have been concerned for years about employee/employer relationships and the protection of employees. They have passed several laws to protect employees, improve their health and safety, and provide minimum employee benefits. Figure 24-4 summarizes major employment laws. HR departments are responsible for understanding the laws and ensuring that the business complies with their requirements.

■ EQUAL OPPORTUNITY IN EMPLOYMENT

In recent years, many businesses have taken positive steps to correct discrimination in employment. Those steps include the development of written plans for fair employment practices, a review of recruitment and selection procedures, improved access to job training to qualify employees for promotions who may have been excluded in the past, diversity training for all managers and employees, and improved performance evaluation procedures that reduce bias. Companies that have taken a sincere and active interest in improving the diversity of their workforce and eliminating discrimination have found that diversity improves decision making by bringing a rich array of ideas and perspectives to company planning and problem-solving.

■ CHANGES IN PROVIDING HUMAN RESOURCES SERVICES

Companies are looking at ways to improve HR services while controlling the costs of providing those services. They are finding many ways to use technology to reduce paperwork and streamline the process of maintaining and distributing information to employees. Some companies are also employing outside companies to perform some HRM tasks.

USE OF TECHNOLOGY Managing human resources requires a great deal of information pertaining to every employee in the organization. Much of the cost of HRM goes into the paperwork needed to gather and update this information. Employees must fill out forms. Then HR employees must make copies, store them, and retrieve them when needed. Whenever a change occurs, the process must be repeated.

Computers have greatly improved the way companies gather and store employment information. Companies now store employment data electronically, making access and updates easy. When an employee

LAW AND PURPOSE

FIGURE 24-4

Laws Providing Benefits and
Protection for Employees

OCCUPATIONAL SAFETY AND HEALTH ACT

The law developed very specific safety and health standards for businesses. The Department of Labor enforces those standards through inspections of businesses and investigations of accidents.

FAIR LABOR STANDARDS ACT

The Act established a minimum wage that must be paid to employees by those businesses included in the law. The businesses must pay employees 1 ½ times their normal wage rate for any hours above 40 worked in a week. The law places limits on the number of hours and times during the day when teenagers can work. It also prevents businesses from hiring people under 18 years old to work in hazardous occupations.

SOCIAL SECURITY ACT

The portion of the Social Security Act that provides pensions to retired workers and their families and provides benefits to disabled workers is known as Old Age, Survivors, and Disability Insurance. Medicare is a broad program of hospital and health insurance for people who have reached retirement age.

UNEMPLOYMENT INSURANCE

Unemployment insurance provides a fund to pay an income to certain unemployed workers. The unemployment insurance program is administered by each state. To be eligible for unemployment benefits, a worker must not be responsible for losing the job and must be actively looking for new employment.

WORKERS' COMPENSATION

All states have workers' compensation laws that require employers to provide insurance for death, injury, or illness resulting from employment.

CIVIL RIGHTS ACT OF 1964

This act prohibits discrimination in hiring, training, and promotion on the basis of race, color, gender, religion, or national origin.

EQUAL PAY ACT

This act prohibits unequal pay for men and women doing substantially similar work.

AMERICANS WITH DISABILITIES ACT

This act prohibits discrimination on the basis of physical or mental disabilities.

FAMILY AND MEDICAL LEAVE ACT

This act permits workers to take up to 12 weeks of unpaid leave for the birth or adoption of a child and for personal illness or illness of an immediate family member.

MANAGEMENT CLOSE-UP

INCREASING EMPLOYMENT OPPORTUNITIES THROUGH THE ADA

Many companies search to fill increasingly technical and complex jobs with qualified applicants. Some employment divisions report screening hundreds of applications to find one person who meets the necessary job requirements. At the same time, businesses overlook millions of Americans who have necessary job qualifications for many jobs. Why? They have disabilities that many employers believe will prevent them from performing job duties effectively.

Because of misunderstanding, stereotypes, and discrimination faced by disabled Americans in the workplace, a new employment law was enacted in 1990. The Americans with Disabilities Act (ADA) prohibits employment discrimination against individuals with physical and mental handicaps or chronic illnesses, if the applicant is able to perform the basic functions of the job. Under ADA, employers must provide the opportunity for all disabled applicants who are otherwise qualified for the job to compete for available jobs. A qualified applicant is a person who has the required education and experience and can perform the work if the employer provides "reasonable accommodation."

Reasonable accommodation means that the employer must make facilities, equipment, procedures, and activities accessible and usable; restructure jobs and work tasks when possible; and provide access to the same benefits and privileges available to other employees. The word "reasonable" is used to ensure that employers do not have to make changes that result in a severe financial hardship for the business or that alter the job, so that required work cannot be completed. Studies done in businesses in preparation for implementing the ADA found that, with careful planning, many accommodations for disabled employees could be accomplished at no additional cost. Other changes could be made at relatively low cost by implementing creative solutions. While some organizations are concerned about the impact and cost of complying with the Americans with Disabilities Act, others have found that it has encouraged them to consider a group of productive employees they had previously ignored.

THINK CRITICALLY

1. Why do you believe it was necessary for the federal government to pass the ADA legislation?
2. If you were a businessperson, how would you respond to the ADA requirements?
3. Using your school as an example, in what ways have the facilities, equipment, and materials been modified to meet the needs of disabled students, faculty, and staff? Are there areas in the school where other reasonable accommodations can be made?

gets a raise or moves to a new home, HR employees can easily make these changes in the computer system. To keep records confidential, companies take security precautions, such as requiring a password to access employees' files.

The Internet has also made HR activities more efficient. The Internet provides a way for employers and job seekers to exchange information. Companies can use the Internet to communicate new policies or new benefit options to employees throughout the company and the world. Companies may even set up information kiosks in cafeterias and break rooms, so employees can easily check on benefits and other employment information. People participating in employee evaluation, such as the 360-degree feedback process, can complete their evaluation forms online.

OUTSOURCING OF SERVICES   Some companies are now outsourcing some or all of the HR services. As you learned in Chapter 15, *outsourcing* is hiring an outside firm to perform specialized tasks. For example, a company may hire an outside employment agency to perform all of its employment activities, including recruiting, selecting, and even training. A second common use of outsourcing in HRM is to contract with an information systems company to administer all of the data required for managing human resources.

CHAPTER CONCEPTS

- Human resources management consists of all activities involved with acquiring, developing, and compensating the people who do the company's work. The HR department is responsible for maintaining an adequate number of employees and developing fair pay plans that will help keep them satisfied with their jobs and productive. HR managers work with all managers and employees in the company.

- The major activities of an HR department involve employment, wages and benefits, performance improvement, employee relations, health and safety, performance management, employee assistance programs, and employment planning and research.

- The HR department establishes procedures to recruit an adequate pool of qualified people from whom new employees can be selected. HR helps to orient new employees to the company and train them for their new jobs. HR then follows up in a few weeks to see if the selection process resulted in hiring the right person for the job and the person is performing well.

- Human resources plays a role in completing employee promotions, transfers, and releases. HR also helps establish objective criteria for determining who will be promoted, transferred, or released. The procedures must ensure that all employees have the opportunity to qualify for jobs in which they are interested. Replacing lost employees is expensive, so HR tracks employee turnover and tries to determine why people are leaving and attempts to help the company retain good workers.

- Human resources develops pay plans that encourage people to work for the company, while using the company's resources efficiently. Common types of plans are time plans, performance plans, and combination plans. Employees' total compensation includes benefits, such as insurance, vacation time, and pension plans, as well as wages or salaries.

- Computers and the use of the Internet have made information easier to gather, maintain, and make available to people when they need it. To improve services while controlling costs, some companies now outsource HR activities.

BUILD VOCABULARY POWER

Define the following terms and concepts.

1. human resources management (HRM)
2. 360-degree feedback
3. employee assistance programs
4. job description
5. job specification
6. promotion
7. transfer
8. discharge
9. layoff

10. employee turnover	19. employee benefits
11. exit interview	20. profit-sharing plan
12. compensation	21. pension plan
13. wage	22. 401k plan
14. salary	23. IRA plan
15. commission plan	24. Keogh plan
16. piece-rate plan	25. flextime
17. combination plan	26. job sharing
18. bonus	27. cafeteria plan

REVIEW FACTS

1. Why are people such important resources for businesses?
2. What must companies do to begin human resources planning?
3. What are the common human resources services provided by most companies?
4. How is a 360-degree feedback system different from the traditional way of evaluating employee performance?
5. Why are companies adding employee assistance programs to the benefits they offer employees?
6. What are several negative results of poor employee selection procedures?
7. What important sources should companies consider using in order to recruit applicants for a job opening?
8. What types of information should not be included in an employment application form?
9. What activities does the HR department perform when a new employee is hired?
10. Why should a company attempt to keep a good current employee as long as possible rather than hire a new employee?
11. What is the difference between a discharge and a layoff?
12. What are three common types of pay plans?
13. How do employee benefits affect a firm's compensation costs?
14. What advantages does a cafeteria benefits plan offer to employees?
15. Why are some companies outsourcing some or all of their human resources tasks?

DISCUSS IDEAS

1. Which human resources activities are most and least important to a company's management? Which are most and least important to a company's employees? Why?
2. Why should the HR department be involved in recruiting and hiring new employees?
3. Why should applicants be eliminated if they do a poor job of completing the application form?
4. Form two teams to debate this statement: "Employers have a right to do random drug testing of their employees."

5. Why should the company consider alternatives to discharge for employees who are not performing well? Under what circumstances do you think that the company should discharge an employee immediately?

6. What problems may be indicated by a high rate of employee turnover? What are some common reasons that companies might experience a very high employee turnover rate?

7. What are the advantages and disadvantages of time and performance pay plans and what do combination plans do to emphasize advantages and reduce disadvantages of each type?

8. Offer some examples of jobs for which salaries have recently been affected by supply and demand for labor. How should a company respond when it finds that employees are leaving to obtain higher wages and salaries from other companies?

9. What do you believe would be the most important employee benefits to a young, beginning employee? To an experienced, married employee with children? To an older employee nearing retirement? Are there any benefits you believe all three types of employees would value?

10. What steps can a human resources department take to ensure that all people have an equal employment opportunity in the selection and promotion processes?

11. What kinds of protection do current laws afford employees?

ANALYZE INFORMATION

1. A telemarketing firm has a complex pay structure for its salespeople. Each person is given a base salary and a quota (minimum expected sales). In addition to the base salary, the company pays the following commissions on sales:

    4 percent for all sales up to $75,000
    5 percent for sales of $75,001 – $150,000
    6 percent for any sales above $150,000

Any salesperson who exceeds the assigned quota is paid a bonus of $5,000. On a separate sheet of paper, complete the following table using the information given.

Salesperson	Base Salary	Commission	Bonus	Total Salary
Egan				
Ranelle				
Chen				

Egan has a base salary of $20,000, sales of $80,000, and a quota of $75,000.

Ranelle has a base salary of $28,000, sales of $140,000, and a quota of $150,000.

Chen has a base salary of $31,000, sales of $220,000, and a quota of $200,000.

2. Cars-4-U is a new auto dealership owned by Fred Anderson and Julia Parente as a partnership. They are aware that most auto dealerships pay salespeople commissions on sales volume. They know that some customers view salespeople negatively, believing they are willing to do anything to make a sale. Fred and Julia don't want to have dissatisfied customers based on the actions of their salespeople. However, they also know that they need sales to make a profit, so the salespeople must be able to convince prospective customers to buy cars. They are considering several options for paying the salespeople. The options are: (a) to offer an attractive hourly wage, which is not related to sales volume; (b) to offer a small weekly salary and a reasonable commission based on the number of cars sold; (c) to offer an attractive commission based on the total dollar sales generated by the salesperson with no additional salary; and (d) to offer a reasonable monthly salary, a small commission on each car sold, and a bonus based on the satisfaction level of customers after they have purchased a car.

   Discuss the options with a small group of class members. Determine the advantages and disadvantages of each plan in meeting the goals of the partners as well as the needs of prospective salespeople. Consider other possible compensation plans. Report to the class on the plan that your team prefers and why.

3. Go to the Internet and locate an application form for a job. Print the form and fill it out. Which of the questions on the application do you think would be most helpful to the company in deciding whether to hire you? Are there any questions that do not seem useful or that could discriminate against some applicants? Describe the changes and improvements you would make in the application form to improve the selection process.

4. As the human resources manager of a large supermarket, you are responsible for hiring new cashiers. You normally hire two to five new cashiers each month, because this job category has a high turnover rate. Write a job description and specifications for the position. Answer the following questions:

   a. What sources would you use to find qualified applicants?

   b. What procedures would you use to select the new person?

   c. What would you do with a new employee to get him or her successfully started on the job?

   d. How would you reduce the rate of employee turnover?

5. Use the library or the Internet to research the history of the Equal Pay Act or the Family and Medical Leave Act. Describe how the changing composition of the workforce and other social forces led to the law's passage.

6. Form small groups. Each group should visit a different local company. Ask to see the firm's safety and security procedures in action. Take notes and then present your findings to the class.

SOLVE BUSINESS PROBLEMS

CASE 24-1

Charles Morgan was hired five weeks ago to work in the mailroom of the Teletron Trading Corporation. His job was to collect mail twice daily from each office in the building, sort and process outgoing mail, deliver outgoing mail to the post office, and pick up incoming mail from the post office. He learned the job in one day by working with the outgoing employee, Tomika Williams. Tomika had been hired by another company and had only one day left with the company by the time Charles was hired.

After one month, Charles thought that he was doing well. While some of the first few days had been rather rough, things seemed to be going more smoothly now. He rarely saw his supervisor, but when he did the supervisor always had a pleasant greeting.

A week later he received notice that he was being discharged next week at the end of his six-week probationary period. There was no explanation for the discharge, and Charles was not aware of the probationary period. He went to the human resources office immediately. The employment manager pulled a folder from the file and began reading notes that had been placed there during the past month. Charles responded truthfully to each item:

a. An hour late to work on May 15: "My car wouldn't start, but I called to say that I would be in as soon as possible. I worked an extra hour at the end of the day to finish my duties."

b. Two offices complained that the mail had not been picked up on the second of the month: "It was my second day on the job, and I couldn't remember all of the stops. After the second day, I made a schedule and I haven't missed an office since."

c. The Research Department complained that an important document was sent by regular mail when it should have been sent by Express Mail: "I didn't know the policy for deciding when and how to send items until I was told I had done it wrong. I asked the supervisor, who gave me a procedures manual to study. Tomika Williams had not told me about the manual."

Several other similar complaints were included in the file. Charles readily admitted to but explained each one. According to the employment manager, Charles was being discharged in keeping with company policy. The policy stated that any employee who received five or more complaints about work procedures during the probationary period was automatically discharged.

Think Critically:

1. What is your opinion of the company's probationary and discharge policy for new employees? Justify your opinion.
2. Develop several reasons to justify the probationary and discharge policy of the company. Describe what you believe the company should do to improve the policy.
3. Why do you believe Charles was prepared for his job in the way he was? What role should the human resources department play when employees receive that type of training? What recommendations can you make to improve the company's training procedures?

CASE 24-2

Joanne Wilkens and Teresa Soto were exercising on the stationary bicycles in the health and fitness center of the Wainwright Company. As they exercised, they discussed an article that had appeared in the company's on-line newsletter.

Joanne: *The article said that the average employee in the company receives total compensation of $36,500 a year. I can't believe that. I think I'm close to the average in salary, and I'll only take home a little more than $28,000 this year.*

Teresa: *That's right. What they don't say is that we have a lot of money deducted from our checks each month for taxes, insurance, and the cost of the retirement plan.*

Joanne: *As a matter of fact, the article says the company contributes an additional $9,000 on the average for each employee to pay for benefits. That makes over $17,000 difference between what I take home and what the company says I receive in compensation and benefits. I can't imagine what benefits we get that cost that much money. There must be a mistake in those figures.*

Teresa: *Let's go past the Human Resources office when we get finished here. Maybe they can explain the difference.*

Think Critically:

1. If the newsletter information is accurate and if Joanne is paid about the average amount of all employees, how can you justify the difference between the compensation figures?
2. Should employees consider the amount that is taken out of their paychecks each month for taxes, insurance, and pensions as a part of their compensation? Why or why not?
3. Why do you believe that many employees are like Joanne and Teresa and don't recognize the total cost of employee benefits? What should a company do to avoid that problem?
4. If you worked in the human resources department, how would you explain the difference in the salary and benefits the company says it pays and the amount of money Joanne and Teresa take home in their paychecks?

PROJECT: MY BUSINESS, INC.

Because a small business has only a few employees, each employee is very important to the success of the company. When you begin to hire employees for your business, you will need procedures designed to hire excellent employees. You will also need to develop effective human resources policies and procedures that will encourage employees to be productive and help you keep them working for you.

DATA COLLECTION

1. Review the employment ads in your newspaper for several days. Identify ads for employment in small service businesses. Study the qualifications required and descriptions of duties listed.
2. Interview the owner of a small business. Discuss with the owner each of the human resources activities listed Figure 24-1. Identify the problems the business has in managing human resources. Ask the owner if substance abuse among employees is a problem for the business, and how he or she deals with the problem.

3. Investigate Internet resources for checking the backgrounds of job applicants for criminal records. Write down your thoughts about doing these kinds of checks.
4. Obtain and study the security policies of two local businesses. Then write a policy statement to help provide security for your employees.

5. Search the Internet to identify recommendations on benefit plans for small businesses. Sites such as the Small Business Administration and the Department of Labor are excellent starting points for your research.

ANALYSIS

1. Develop a job description and job specifications for an employee you would hire. Then write the copy for a newspaper advertisement you would use to recruit potential employees.
2. Develop a specific set of procedures to follow in hiring and orienting new employees. Include a statement of nondiscrimination in hiring that complies with applicable laws.
3. Identify the advantages and disadvantages of two pay plans you would consider using for employees. Then select the plan you would use and establish the wage or salary rate for full- and part-time employees.
4. Identify the benefits you will provide for employees, including those required by federal and state law and any additional benefits, if any, you will provide. Attempt to calculate the cost of each benefit for one employee.
5. Develop a specific set of procedures to follow for discharging and laying off employees.

EMPLOYEE AND ORGANIZATIONAL DEVELOPMENT

OBJECTIVES

25-1 Define organizational development and discuss the two important components of an organizational development program.

25-2 Explain the components of a career development program.

25-3 Describe the value of performance reviews and training and development to businesses and employees.

25-4 Describe the variety of career opportunities in business, including international business careers.

25-5 Outline the steps in preparing a career plan.

THE END OF AN ERA AT ALLIANCE INDUSTRIES

ames Lane had a good life. Since graduating from high school, he had worked for Alliance Industries, a company that produced steel and steel products for the auto industry. In the 23 years of his employment, he had enjoyed most days of work, had a great group of friends at the company, and earned a comfortable living for his family. His career had progressed at Alliance from a basic maintenance position, to machine operator, and then eight years ago to supervisor of machining. During that time he had completed a two-year technical degree at a community college and recently had enrolled again in two courses to be able to better use computers in his work.

James now faced an important decision. Alliance Industries was being challenged by competition and changes in the auto industry. The industry was changing from the use of steel to other metals and plastics. Changes in technology were requiring companies in the steel industry to acquire new equipment, and competition was forcing cost-cutting. Alliance was reducing its workforce, including the elimination of most supervisory positions. The company offered James the opportunity to go back to a machinist position, but it would require additional training and a slight reduction in pay. James didn't know how he would be accepted if he went back to work with the people he had been supervising and if he would be happy with that work. If he chose not to accept the job change, Alliance would provide career counseling and other services to help him find another job, but there was no guarantee that it would be the type of work James enjoyed.

■ THE NEW EMPLOYMENT ENVIRONMENT

In the last part of the 20th century, many companies faced global competitive pressures unlike those they had seen before. That competition forced companies to reconsider their organizational size, structure, and operations. Many were forced to downsize their operations by cutting the number of employees, reducing product offerings, or cutting costs in other ways. Other companies restructured their operations to work and use resources more efficiently. Some large companies reduced employment by thousands of people. Like the problem facing James Lane with Alliance Industries, employees who had spent many years with the same company (some nearing retirement) suddenly found themselves without a job.

Many former employees who lost their jobs when businesses cut back have been unable to find satisfying employment. Some have had to accept lower-level jobs or jobs that pay less or offer fewer benefits than those they held previously. Those who were able to keep their jobs are not certain of their **job security,** the likelihood that they will continue to be employed by the same company in the future. They may distrust their employer, believing that the actions of businesses demonstrate a lack of commitment to employees.

Now in the 21st century, the focus is on developing a whole new generation of businesses. The Internet has led to the creation of many new organizations that look quite different from traditional businesses. They may have only a few employees, and the employees may not work in the same building or even in the same city. The Internet companies may rely on other businesses to perform many of the traditional business functions, and the owners may have more skill and experience with technology than with organizing and managing a business.

Today, we see dramatic changes in both traditional and new businesses. Dealing with the result of those changes presents challenges to both employees and managers. Much of the pressure to maintain a strong organization falls on the human resources department. Whether it is a traditional business that has gone through a major restructuring or a new business attempting to build a unique type of organization, human resources personnel must help the organization be effective.

Two major responsibilities have emerged for the human resources department in today's organizations. **Organizational development** refers to carefully planned changes in the structure and operation of a business to adjust to a competitive business environment. **Career development** is a program that matches the career plans of employees with the employment needs of the business. This chapter focuses on these two human resources programs. You will learn how companies can make changes in the way the business is organized while maintaining positive management/employee relations. You will also learn about the roles of employee performance reviews and training programs in achieving business and employee goals. Finally, you will examine how individuals can take responsibility for their own career development through effective career planning.

■ ORGANIZATIONAL DEVELOPMENT

Consider all of the ways that employees can contribute to the success or failure of a business. Employees play a major role in product quality, customer satisfaction, equipment maintenance, and efficient use of materials to limit waste. You can probably think of many other ways that employees can help or hurt the business for which they work.

The ways businesses organize work and provide resources also affect their success. Inefficient work processes, delays in receiving needed resources, and problems within channels of distribution all hinder a business's ability to meet customer needs. Because of such problems, companies are now paying a great deal of attention to the way in which they structure their organization, how work flows through the business, and how employees work together and with their managers. Today, businesses are using organizational development programs to make sure they continue to be successful.

Two important elements of an effective organizational development program are making improvements in work processes and building effective working relationships. Improving work processes means improving the way work is accomplished in a business. The goal of work process improvement is to eliminate errors, improve quality, and reduce costs.

The focus of the second element of organizational development is on the people who complete the work. Studies have shown that employees who believe they are an important part of the organization will be committed to its success and will work to achieve the company's goals. Several important relationships contribute to an effective organization. They are the relationships among a company's personnel, including management-employee relationships, and relationships with people in other organizations with whom the company works and with the company's customers.

■ IMPROVING WORK PROCESSES

One of the focuses of organizational development is to improve the way work is accomplished. This includes the materials and resources used, the organizational structure and relationships among work units, the job duties assigned to individuals and groups, as well as work procedures and operations. Most of the emphasis on improving work processes is directed inside the company. But improving work processes also involves the way businesses work with each other as a part of product development and distribution.

Improving the way work is accomplished may require using new technologies, rearranging work space, changing relationships between departments and work groups, and modifying procedures for completing tasks. Remember the concerns James Lane had about the changes Alliance Industries was planning. The company was changing to new products, equipment, and procedures that would be quite different from what he and other employees had experienced.

It is not easy for any company to make these types of changes when people are used to the older ways of accomplishing work and are reluctant to use new technologies or to change the way they have been doing things for many years. It may even be difficult to identify new ways to organize and accomplish work, because people in the company are familiar only with the way things have been done in the past. Often organizational development programs will bring in experts from outside the company to help identify and study new work processes.

■ IDENTIFYING THE NEED FOR CHANGE

The history of business is filled with many organizations that experienced years of success, only to fall on hard times and ultimately fail. The cause of the business failure may be that competitors were able to make improvements in their products and services, customers did not receive the service they expected, costs were not controlled, or the organizational structure did not adjust to new conditions. No matter what the specific cause, the reason for the failure of previously successful businesses is most likely to be the inability to change. It

BUSINESS INNOVATION

IDEAS FOR SALE

Since most businesses are faced with the need to change, it is not surprising that people are starting new businesses to help other businesses manage change. One of the most unusual new businesses is one that sells ideas.

The BrainStore in Biel, Switzerland is one of those businesses. Its owners refer to their business as an idea factory. In fact, they believe companies can't rely on the typical way that new ideas are generated. The "great idea," a simple brainstorming session, or just thinking about a problem will not achieve the needed results when businesses are faced almost daily with problems and challenges. The BrainStore has moved the process of idea generation into a specific sequence of activities.

The process starts in the *creativity lab.* The lab is an open room with pens, paper, scissors, crayons, beads, and other "toys." These are the tools that support creativity. The room looks more like an elementary school classroom than a place where business people meet. The atmosphere encourages play, experiments, and "completely unrealistic thoughts." The result is usually a large number of creative ideas that can then be processed through the idea factory. The next step in the idea sequence is *compression,* where ideas are sorted, compared, and narrowed to the few judged as best. Then the idea moves through *testing,* where research is completed to determine if the idea will work and can be implemented. Often models or prototypes of solutions will be built for review and further testing. The final step is called *finishing.* Here the idea that has been successfully tested will be prepared for implementation. That may include developing marketing and communications strategies for the organization that will implement the idea or the actual development of products, services, or processes that will support the needed change or solve the problem.

Initially the BrainStore worked with large businesses to create new products, develop marketing programs, or solve challenging problems. However, the owners now believe their ideas can help individual consumers as well, so they have opened a retail version of the business. At a cost of under $20, they will provide help with home decorating ideas, improving personal relationships, or creative ideas for an important speech.

THINK CRITICALLY

1. Do you believe ideas can actually be developed in the same way that a company might manufacture a product? Why or why not?
2. What are the advantages of creating a room that looks like an elementary school classroom for the first step in idea generation? How do you think the results would be different if the company used a typical business office for that activity?
3. Why do you believe individuals would pay $20 to a business that only gives them help with ideas?
4. After working with the BrainStore, what other activities should an organization complete to implement the ideas that were developed?

Source: *Fast Company, April, 2000*

may be that the executives of the company did not recognize the need for change, believed the successful company did not need to change, or were unable to plan and manage the needed change.

Throughout this textbook you have learned that the environment faced by businesses today is very different from that in the past. Those differences occur both outside the business (the *external environment*) and inside the business (the *internal environment*). Today, the external factors that are most likely to result in problems for an organization are changes in workforce demographics, the nature of competition, customer expectations, and technology. Several important internal factors that affect a company's success are quite similar. They include changes in the makeup of the company's workforce, employee expectations, outdated work processes and technology, ineffective organizational structure, and poor management practices.

Figure 25-1 shows several key indicators that an organization may be experiencing problems requiring major change. Every organization should pay careful attention to its external and internal environment to identify changes in any of those indicators. Major changes in any of the indicators may suggest growing problems that should lead to plans for organizational development.

When a business tries to solve a problem, it often discovers that the problem results from a fundamental flaw in the operations of the business. Organizational development programs must identify and resolve the underlying operational problem in order to fix the original problem.

For example, one company found that production levels had declined significantly during June, July, and August. As company managers studied the problem, they discovered that employee absences were almost double on Mondays and Fridays than on the other days of the week. Production was delayed on both of those days because work teams were not full or temporary employees brought in on those

- **New competitors entering the market**
- **Introduction of new technologies by other businesses**
- **Changes in laws and regulations affecting the business**
- **Major changes in products and services offered or in markets served**
- **Rapid growth by the business**
- **Loss of market share**
- **Increasing customer complaints**
- **Poor relationships with business partners**
- **Increasing operating costs**
- **Decreasing revenues or profits**
- **Decline in employee morale and increasing employee turnover**
- **Conflicts among departments or other work units**
- **Participation in a merger or acquisition**

FIGURE 25-1

Important Indicators that Organizations Need to Make Changes

days were not as efficient. In order to solve the production problem, the employee absence issue had to be resolved. Working with employees, the managers discovered that the way vacation days were scheduled encouraged employees to use Mondays and Fridays to have short summer vacations. A revised policy allowed employees to schedule two- or three-day vacations in the middle of the week. This change reduced Monday and Friday absences and solved the production problem.

Another company experienced an increasing number of customer complaints regarding late deliveries of products. The company had used the same parcel delivery service to make deliveries to customers for over 20 years. A study of the problem revealed that the delivery company had changed its distribution procedures. It was using larger trucks and making few trips to many cities to cut its costs. To improve customer service, the company stopped using that parcel service and contracted with a new, smaller delivery company that used a computerized delivery scheduling system. This change allowed the company to schedule product delivery with customers when they made the purchase and reduced late deliveries by more than 80 percent. Fixing the underlying delivery service problem resolved the issue of customer complaints.

■ PLANNING AN ORGANIZATIONAL DEVELOPMENT PROGRAM

As soon as the company identifies a problem or need for change, it should plan and implement an organizational development program. Since almost all important changes in a business involve or affect employees, the human resources department should have an important role in the program. The changes may involve developing new employee skills or increasing or decreasing the size of the workforce. A change or major reorganization may affect management/employee relationships. The company may decide to change the pay or benefits plans to encourage employee participation or to reduce costs.

The major steps in planning and implementing an organizational development program are the following:

1. *Affirm the mission and goals of the organization.* There needs to be agreement within the company about the purpose of the business and the criteria to be used to determine if the company is successful. A company should not easily change its mission or goals but may need to change them in response to the external and internal environment.

2. *Identify the important markets that will be the company's primary focus and the products and services needed to serve those markets.* This step will require establishing customer service standards. In Chapter 13, you learned that a *standard* is a specific measure against which something is judged. **Customer service standards,** then, are measures against which the company judges its performance in meeting customer expectations. Those standards may include the mini-

mum acceptable levels of product quality, delivery speed, order-fulfillment accuracy, and customer support and follow-up.

3. *Determine the organizational changes required to achieve the company's mission, goals, and customer service standards, and prepare a plan for implementing the changes.* These will usually involve one or more of the following factors: work processes, the organizational structure, work relationships, and employee skills. Also, the plan should include **performance standards,** which are specific statements of the expected results from critical business activities. Most organizational development changes require a long time to achieve success. Implementation may take many months, and the company may not see results for a year or more.

4. *Build commitment within the organization for the changes.* Successful organizational change requires the understanding and support of managers and employees. That understanding and support will occur only if all employees are fully informed of (1) the change, (2) the reasons change is necessary, (3) the likely results if the changes are not made, (4) how they will be affected by the change, and (5) how the organization and its employees will benefit if the change is successful. Successful organizational development usually results when company personnel are involved early in the process and when they have a role in designing the plan.

5. *Follow through on the organizational development plans.* Employees are more likely to support the plans if they see that the organization is committed to them and that change is occurring. Managers should keep employees informed of results of the changes even if

ILLUSTRATION 25-1

How can a company build commitment within the organization for changes?

they are not always positive at the beginning. Unless something occurs that makes it clear that the plan will not work, the organizational development plan should continue until it achieves the goals.

6. *Make the new process part of the organization's culture.* If people believe the change is not important or is only temporary, they will not commit to its success. When the new process is implemented and supported, the organization has changed, and the old procedures are no longer appropriate, the organizational development program is complete.

Alliance Industries, discussed in the opening scenario, needed to implement an organizational development program for the major changes they were planning. Can you find evidence that Alliance used any of the six steps you just studied?

■ IMPROVING THE WORK ENVIRONMENT

The needs and expectations of workers today are very different from those of workers in the past. Work is just one part of an employee's life. Of course, employees want jobs that provide a reasonable wage or salary. But the amount of money earned is not always the most important thing. Today, employees are concerned about a variety of factors related to their work, including the work schedule and working conditions. Vacations, insurance, pensions, and other benefits are also important to most people. They also want an interesting and challenging job as well as recognition for their work. Both personal and financial needs are important to employees, and managers must recognize those needs in order to maintain an effective workforce.

Satisfied employees are more productive, have fewer absences, and are more likely to want to stay with the company. Therefore, managers spend considerable time working with employees to make the work environment as satisfying as possible. Studies have found that employees are most satisfied with their work when they (1) perform interesting work, (2) feel responsible for the work, (3) receive recognition for good work, and (4) have a feeling of achievement.

These results show that employees are concerned with many things other than the amount of their paycheck and benefits like vacation days. It is surprising to many managers that while the amount of compensation is important, it is not necessarily more important than other factors related to the job. Because of those studies, companies are directing their organizational development efforts toward the design of the work environment and jobs to better meet employee needs. **Job design** refers to the kinds of tasks that make up a job and the way workers perform these tasks in doing their jobs.

Organizations try to make work more meaningful and motivating for employees. One way to do this is through **job enlargement,** which means making a job more interesting by adding variety to the tasks. For example, three workers on an assembly line might be responsible

Exam 4
? 1

for three separate tasks, each one performing one task over and over. With job enlargement, each worker is given responsibility to complete all three tasks. In this way they can perform a greater variety of tasks, making the work less monotonous and boring. Also, the company now has three people who can perform all of the work rather than three specialized employees who can perform only one part of a complex job.

Employees should be involved in making the decision to change the job and in redesigning the job. Employees also need training and adequate time and practice to develop the new skills. Companies should not enlarge jobs just to reduce the number of employees or to get employees to do more work. If employees believe that these are the real reasons for enlarging their jobs, they will not accept the changes willingly.

Another use of job design to increase employee effectiveness and motivation is cross training. With **cross training,** employees are trained to perform more than one job in the company, even though they typically perform only one. Employees can be rotated to other jobs when an absence or illness occurs, while a replacement employee is being trained, when a significant increase or decrease in the amount of work occurs for a specific job, or simply to provide change and variety for employees. Cross training makes an employee more valuable to the company since that person can perform a broader set of work tasks. Employees learn more about the work performed in the organization as they learn multiple jobs and increase their skills.

Another way to use job design to improve employee satisfaction is to involve employees in decision making. **Job enrichment** means giving employees the authority to make meaningful decisions about their work. For example, managers may allow workers to make choices about how to do their jobs. Managers may ask employees for advice on how to improve performance or how to reduce errors. Job responsibilities may be changed so employees can solve problems themselves, without checking with their supervisor. For example, in one major hotel chain, employees are authorized to immediately take the necessary steps to resolve a customer problem or complaint at a cost of up to $200 without consulting a manager.

As you learned in earlier chapters, some companies have work teams that are responsible for the entire assembly of a product, performance of a service, or operation of a small unit in the business. The team helps with goal setting, shares all tasks, and is responsible for the results. Companies using this system have found that team members develop a strong loyalty with the other members and take personal responsibility for the effective operation of the team and the quality of its work. An improved work environment and worker involvement are important goals of organizational development.

Improving management and employee relationships, making work more meaningful, and developing effective work teams are all important organizational development programs. They affect the internal

FACTS AND FIGURES

Employers who tap into their employees' need to grow in their jobs are more likely to retain talented people. An employer should *set a direction* for each employee that is in alignment with the firm's vision statement; *listen* to the employee's ideas about how he or she can help the company meet its goals; *guide* the employee in meeting the business's goals; and *measure and give feedback* through evaluations.

environment of the business. In addition, some organizational development programs work to improve relationships in the external environment, including the way employees interact with other businesses in the distribution channel and with customers. Many businesses involve personnel from cooperating businesses in solving problems and developing new procedures. They frequently consult customers in order to consider their needs and perceptions in planning organizational changes.

■ CAREER DEVELOPMENT

In the past, many companies were quite short-sighted when they planned for their employment needs. When a position was vacant, they would begin the recruitment and selection process. If they no longer needed employees, they might terminate those employees without considering future employment needs. Those procedures were based on the belief that companies could easily find the employees they needed. Those companies did not view employees as a particularly valuable resource.

Successful businesses view their relationships with employees very differently today. They realize that it is not easy to find employees with the qualifications required. It is also very expensive to hire and train a new employee. Companies invest in employees and want to get the greatest value from them. That occurs when companies hire employees with skills that closely match the needs of the job, train them, and then keep them happy, so they will stay with the company for a long time. The companies with this new philosophy recognize that the knowledge and performance of their employees are major factors in their success.

Changing technology requires employees to update their skills. For example, not many years ago, businesses processed most information manually, using typewriters and calculators. Today, companies process information with computers. Auto mechanics used to rely on hand tools and their own knowledge and observational skills to repair automobiles. Now they have access to a variety of electronic tools, machines, and computerized diagnostic equipment. Every business has similar examples of new skills that are required of employees. It is not possible to be successful with the old equipment and old skills. To get the needed skills, businesses offer training to current employees when new technology requires it and search for new employees with up-to-date skills to fill vacancies.

In the scenario at the beginning of the chapter, James Lane had been a very valuable employee to Alliance Industries for many years. Even though the company was undergoing major changes, it was attempting to include James in its plans by offering him another job and the needed training to prepare for that job.

ILLUSTRATION 25-2

How can businesses help their employees update their skills?

■ REQUIREMENTS FOR A CAREER DEVELOPMENT PROGRAM

A **career development program** is a plan for meeting the company's future employment needs by systematically preparing current employees for future positions in the company. While human resources personnel will be responsible for implementing the career development program, they will need the support of all parts of the company for the program to be successful. A career development program requires a long-term organizational plan, career paths, effective employee performance reviews, career counseling, and training and development for employees.

LONG-TERM PLANS Career development starts with the job opportunities in a company. Companies need to determine what jobs will be available in the future, how many people will be needed in each job, and the knowledge and skills those employees will require. In the previous section, you learned that companies study their external and internal environments to identify business opportunities and needed changes in the organization. One part of that study includes employment needs. Then the HR department can work with that information to project specific job opportunities in each part of the company and the requirements employees must meet for each job.

CAREER PATHS A **career path** is a progression of related jobs with increasing skill requirements and responsibility. Career paths provide opportunities for employees to advance within the company, to make additional contributions, and to receive increased satisfaction from their work.

- Exam 4
? 15

Traditionally, career paths moved an employee from an entry-level position into management. However, companies also offer career paths that allow employees to advance into non-management positions. Some people do not want to be managers, and companies usually have relatively few management positions. Therefore, companies often make other opportunities available, so that employees do not get locked into one job if they choose not to become a manager or are unable to qualify for a management position. Examples of a management career path and a non-management path are shown in Figure 25-2.

Companies should identify a variety of career paths. Each job should be a part of a career path, and employees should be aware of the paths available to them from the job they currently hold.

PERFORMANCE REVIEWS Employees and managers need accurate information on the skills and abilities of each employee to make effective career decisions. When employees know how well they are performing, they can determine what skills they need to improve to meet the current job requirements or to qualify for another job in a career path. In an effective career development program, managers carefully evaluate employees' performance and regularly review the information with

FIGURE 25-2

Examples of Management and Non-Management Career Paths

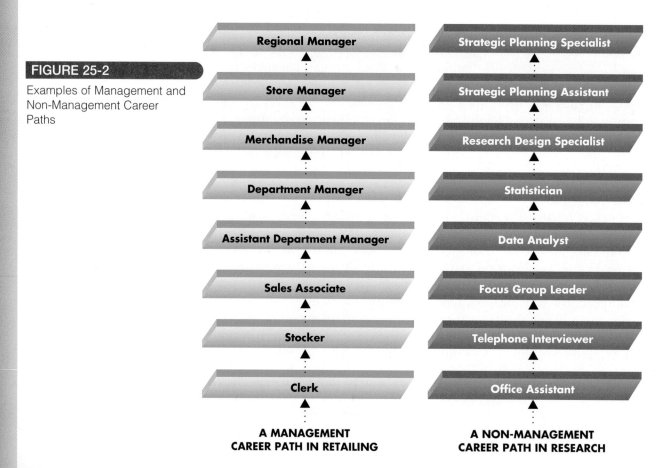

A MANAGEMENT CAREER PATH IN RETAILING	A NON-MANAGEMENT CAREER PATH IN RESEARCH
Regional Manager	Strategic Planning Specialist
Store Manager	Strategic Planning Assistant
Merchandise Manager	Research Design Specialist
Department Manager	Statistician
Assistant Department Manager	Data Analyst
Sales Associate	Focus Group Leader
Stocker	Telephone Interviewer
Clerk	Office Assistant

the employee. With that information, the manager and employee can determine whether the employee needs additional training to improve performance and to prepare to advance in the organization. The results of performance reviews should be compared to new job requirements as the company makes changes, so that employees know what is expected of them.

CAREER COUNSELING   For career development to be effective, employees must be aware of opportunities and plan their career paths. The HR department offers career information and counseling services as a part of the career development program. Many companies have made career counseling part of every employee's performance review conference. Managers are often trained to provide career information to the employees they supervise.

Career counseling may result in an individual career plan. A **career plan** identifies the jobs that are part of the employee's career path, the training and development needed to advance along the career path, and a tentative schedule for the plan's activities. The plan is jointly developed by the employee, a human resources specialist, and possibly the employee's manager.

Some companies have career centers. **Career centers** are facilities where human resources employees manage career development activities. Employees can visit the center to obtain career information (computer programs, Internet sites, books, pamphlets, films, etc.), visit with career counselors, and schedule career planning workshops or testing as they prepare for new jobs.

TRAINING AND DEVELOPMENT   The final part of a career development program is training employees in the skills needed for changing job requirements and new jobs. With careful planning, companies can develop training programs and other educational opportunities to prepare employees for new job requirements before the need arises. In that way, the business can be assured that it will have well-trained employees to fill job needs and employees will know they can get the training necessary for job changes.

■ IMPLEMENTING A CAREER DEVELOPMENT PROGRAM

Career planning does not just happen. It also cannot be considered the responsibility of employees alone. Businesses that want to match employees and jobs successfully must do several things to ensure that the career development program works well.

First, responsibility for organizing and managing the career development program must be assigned. Most companies assign the program to the human resources department. The HR department will put together the people, materials, and procedures needed for the program.

Second, everyone in the business must be educated about the career development program and his or her role in career planning. Managers need to identify career opportunities in their departments and work with HR personnel when changes are planned in their departments that will affect the career plans of employees. Managers also have specific responsibilities in a career development program. They evaluate employee performance and include career planning in follow-up conferences. They help identify employees who are ready for career advancement. They serve as coaches and mentors for their employees to help each worker make effective career choices.

Employees need to be aware of career development resources and how the career planning process works. They are responsible for much of their individual career planning and development but need to know where to get help when needed. Employees use performance reviews and evaluation conferences to gather information to make career plans. They can then schedule assessments, counseling, and training to prepare for career advancement.

■ SPECIAL CAREER DEVELOPMENT PROGRAMS

Companies that offer career development programs should make the services available to all employees from the newest to the most experienced. However, there are situations where specific individuals or groups of employees participate in programs designed to meet specific needs in the company. Those programs may not be available to all employees.

Most large businesses offer career planning, training, and counseling to employees selected to be managers. These employees receive testing services, obtain experience in all parts of the business, and often are assigned to an experienced manager who serves as a role model and mentor.

Non-management jobs can be targeted for specific career development programs as well. For example, many jobs are more frequently held by men than women or women than men. Companies may make extra efforts to encourage and prepare people from the under-represented gender for those jobs. Some companies may have difficulty finding qualified candidates for certain jobs. Those positions may be targeted for career development attention. Employees who are interested in or have the knowledge and skills to qualify for hard-to-fill jobs will be encouraged to participate in the special programs. For example, if a company is having difficulty recruiting and hiring computer programmers, it may undertake a career development program to encourage current employees to complete the necessary training for the programming jobs.

■ IMPROVING EMPLOYEE PERFORMANCE

Companies depend on effective and satisfied employees. Just as a company cannot operate if equipment is outdated or regularly needs repair,

FACTS AND FIGURES

Management experts believe that employees have a responsibility for their own performance management, and cite the following areas on which employees should focus: (1) committing to goal achievement; (2) soliciting performance feedback and coaching; (3) communicating openly and regularly with the manager; (4) collecting and sharing performance data; and (5) preparing for performance reviews.

it must have employees with up-to-date skills who perform their jobs accurately and efficiently. Two requirements for maintaining a quality workforce are an effective system for performance review and well-designed training and development programs.

■ PERFORMANCE REVIEW PROCEDURES

Companies must make sure employees are performing as well as they possibly can. A **performance review** is the process of assessing how well employees are doing their jobs. Companies use the information obtained from performance reviews for career planning, determining increases in wages and salaries, and planning training programs.

The first step in developing a performance review process is to determine what to evaluate. Each job should have a complete description of duties and performance expectations, and the review should focus on these duties and expectations. Next, the HR department prepares forms and procedures for performance reviews. Those materials should be designed to make the review process as easy and objective as possible.

Managers conduct formal performance reviews of all employees usually once or twice a year. The manager fills out an evaluation form about the employee's performance. The process in many companies also requires the employee to complete a self-evaluation using the same form. The manager and employee then meet to discuss the results in a performance review conference.

In addition to the formal reviews, employees can conduct self-assessments or ask managers, co-workers, or career counselors to provide feedback. These performance reviews are usually informal but can be very helpful to the employees in understanding how well they are performing their jobs and what needs to be done to improve performance or to prepare for new jobs in a career path.

An upcoming performance evaluation

ILLUSTRATION 25-3

What methods can a manager use to make the performance evaluation meeting a positive experience?

FACTS AND FIGURES

Like most hotel chains, Days Inn of America suffers tremendous employee turnover—around 120 percent a year for hourly employees. The chain has begun using an interactive Web-based training program that teaches the specific skills employees need and provides self-paced learning, testing, and tracking. Experts believe that such technology-based training can result in a 50 percent reduction in time and cost over classroom training.

Exam & ? .14

meeting is often a source of anxiety for both managers and employees. However, if carefully planned, the evaluation meeting can be a positive experience. The following guidelines for managers can help in achieving that goal:

1. Schedule enough time for the discussion and plan for it in advance by reviewing the employee's job requirements and career plan.
2. Focus the discussion on the employee's performance, not on the employee. Feedback should be based on objective information, not opinions.
3. Discuss strengths as well as areas that need improvement. Identify how the strengths can contribute to the employee's career goals and specific ways the employee can develop needed skills and improve performance.

■ PLANNING TRAINING AND DEVELOPMENT

Businesses spend a great deal of money on activities designed to improve the productivity of their employees. Studies estimate that U.S. companies spend $50–60 billion each year on formal training programs. Informal training (i.e., learning on the job, self study, coaching) may cost businesses as much as an additional $200 billion each year. Beyond the costs of training, many companies pay some or all of the costs of college courses that employees take as part of career development programs or as an employee benefit. The large amount of money for training and development can be justified if the result is employees who are able to perform more and higher quality work.

As companies recognize the value of training, they are working to develop more effective training procedures. On the average, companies spend several hundred dollars on every employee each year for training. Therefore, they want to be sure the training is effective in improving employees' performance. Trainers use many techniques to improve employee performance. Figure 25-3 summarizes several characteristics of effective training.

An important activity for all companies is determining the need for employee training. Some training needs are quite obvious. When the company buys new equipment, begins new operations, or introduces improved procedures, employees need to be trained for the changes. Typically, when new employees are hired or experienced employees are promoted to new jobs, they do not have all of the skills needed to begin work immediately. In these cases, companies should offer the needed training.

Other training needs are not as obvious. In some instances, poor work performance can be a symptom of insufficient training. Conflicts among employees, areas of customer dissatisfaction, or work hazards and employee injuries signal the need for training. Unless companies are aware of problems and try to determine whether training can help solve them, the problems likely will not disappear.

TO BE EFFECTIVE, TRAINING SHOULD:

1. Be interesting to the trainee.
2. Be related to knowledge the trainee already has developed.
3. Explain why as well as how something is done.
4. Progress from simple to more difficult steps.
5. Let the trainee learn complicated procedures in small steps.
6. Allow plenty of practice time.
7. Let the trainee concentrate on becoming comfortable with a new procedure before worrying about accuracy.
8. Provide regular and positive feedback to the trainee on progress being made.
9. Be done in short time blocks using a variety of activities.
10. Involve the learner in training activities as much as possible.

FIGURE 25-3

Characteristics of Effective Training Programs

In some companies, each department has formed a problem-solving group made up of managers and employees. Those groups can be used to identify training needs in addition to their other responsibilities. Because they work regularly with the equipment and the procedures of the department, the groups are in a good position to identify performance problems and to help design training.

CAREER OPPORTUNITIES IN BUSINESS

Business careers are appealing because of the number and variety of jobs available and opportunities for advancement. No matter what your interests, skills, or level of education and experience, there is a job in business that matches. Once you have obtained your first job, many opportunities open up. You can advance with additional education or with continuing experience and training on the job.

You can identify career paths in almost any business. If you begin work in a clerical position, you may progress to more specialized jobs in information management or office administration. You can then advance from assistant manager to department manager or a highly specialized position in either area. Some people even progress to the very top of the company as executives. Similar career paths are available to people who begin as counter workers in fast-food restaurants, production workers in factories, or reservation clerks in hotels.

Because common areas of knowledge and skills are important to many types of businesses, you are not limited to one career path, one type of business, or one geographic area. People who begin in banking may change to an insurance career. Someone who is a salesperson for a computer-products company may decide to move to a building-materials company for an increase in salary or more responsibilities. If job prospects are not particularly good in one part of the country, a skilled businessperson can probably find employment in another region. Career paths in business are usually very flexible.

■ LEVELS OF EMPLOYMENT

When you first enter the workforce, you will most likely begin in an entry-level position. You may even get your first job when you are still in high school and have no experience and little understanding of business operations. The top positions in large corporations are held by people with many years of experience. Executives usually have worked in several areas of the business and often have experience in several businesses. Most business executives today have a college degree and, increasingly, graduate degrees.

Businesses have several levels of employment, based on the amount of education and experience required. Common levels are entry, career, specialist, management, and executive/entrepreneur.

Entry-level occupations usually involve routine activities and require little training. These jobs are open to people with little or no previous business education or experience. If you have not worked in business before, this is where you might begin. People hold entry-level jobs for only a short time until they have developed enough experience and skill for promotion. Examples of entry-level jobs are cashier, counter person, clerk, receptionist, and operator.

Career-level jobs require more complex duties. People in *career-level occupations* have the authority to control some of their work and make some decisions. To be successful, they should have a basic understanding of business and skills in the areas in which they are working. They usually view their work as more than a job and have an interest in the area of business as a potential career. Career-level jobs include sales associate, reservations agent, word processor, bank teller, and customer service representative.

Specialist occupations require a variety of skills in one or more business functions and extensive understanding of the operations of a specific company or industry. Specialists are the people considered the most skilled or expert in the activities they complete on the job.

CYBER COMMUNICATION

Besides e-mail, another important source of communication on the Internet is newsgroups. A newsgroup is formed by a group of people who are interested in a particular subject. These groups can be formal or informal. While some are created for entertainment, others are devoted to the exchange of knowledge about a topic.

As with the Internet in general, newsgroups are visited by all sorts of people. Sometimes, freedom of speech conflicts with common courtesy. Since postings can be read by thousands of participants, it's important to be concise and considerate in your messages. It's also wise to exercise caution when participating in newsgroups, and remember not to give out personal information that could cause problems for you later.

ACTIVITY Using library or Internet resources, research the topic of banning newsgroups that have "offensive" content. Is this censorship? Is it a violation of First Amendment rights? Prepare a one-page report on your thoughts about this topic.

Specialists in businesses include buyers, researchers, Web designers, programmers, analysts, professional salespeople, technicians, machine operators, and similar technical or skilled positions.

— Exam 4
? 9.

Supervisors/managers hold the first levels of management positions in companies. They must have a high level of knowledge in the parts of the organization that they supervise. They also must be effective decision-makers and have strong leadership ability. *Supervisor/management occupations* are responsible for specific units in a business and must make decisions about operations and personnel. The job titles associated with this level of employment are supervisor, assistant manager, and manager. The people who perform management tasks on work teams are often called *team leaders*.

Executives/entrepreneurs perform all of the management tasks associated with owning a business or managing a major function, a large unit in a company, or the entire company. People who work in *executive/entrepreneur occupations* are fully responsible for the success or failure of the company. They must possess a comprehensive understanding of business and management. They will spend most of their time planning and evaluating the work of the organization. The positions held by executives/entrepreneurs are vice president, president, chief executive, and owner.

■ CAREERS IN INTERNATIONAL BUSINESS

The growth of trade between countries and increasing global competition provide continuing evidence of the importance of international business. It has never been easier to travel to other countries, communicate with people around the world, buy products produced in other places, and sell products and services abroad. The Internet makes access to almost any business and millions of customers only a mouse-click away. We are members of a global community generally, and a global business community specifically. As businesses expand into international markets, so do the opportunities for international business careers.

International business careers have all of the advantages of a career in one country plus more. In addition to the excitement and challenges that accompany work in any business career, international careers usually offer additional job choices and the chance to develop new skills, travel, and interact with a wide variety of people from different cultures. You learned about many of the requirements to prepare for a career in international business in Chapter 4.

You will recall that the international businessperson needs to know something about the culture of the country in which the business will operate or to which the company's products and service are directed. The economic environment of countries is another important area of study. Currently, English is the international language of business. However, there is no substitute for understanding the language of the

ILLUSTRATION 25-4

What advantages do international business careers have?

country in which you will work. People are favorably impressed when you take the trouble to learn their language. It is difficult to predict which languages will be the most important in your future. Your commitment to study and learn a second language will impress employers as well as your international contacts. You will also find it easier to learn an additional language if needed later. Your selection of international courses in high school and college, travel opportunities, and interactions with people from other countries and cultures are all valuable experiences if you would like to work in international business.

■ PREPARING FOR A BUSINESS CAREER

Preparing for a career in business may seem like trying to negotiate a maze. People who are not familiar with business may have difficulty determining what preparation they need and how to obtain the job they want.

If you talk to people who have worked in business for many years, you will find that some did not plan or prepare for the job they currently hold. They often ended up there after starting in another part of the business or in an entirely different occupation.

Today, a person is less likely to enter a business career without specific preparation. In your study of business, you have seen that a business career requires a great deal of knowledge and skill in a number of areas. People who understand the requirements and carefully plan to develop the necessary skills are more likely to succeed in business. In some ways, preparing for a business career is complicated, but in other ways it is really quite simple. It is often a matter of matching your personal qualities, education, and experience with a career path in business.

Good business education programs exist in high schools as well as in community and junior colleges and vocational/technical schools.

Business is usually one of the largest degree programs in colleges and universities. You can complete a general business preparation or specialize in specific areas, such as accounting, computer science, marketing, or even e-commerce. Many businesses offer education and training programs for their employees or pay for some or all of the costs of college coursework. You can also attend conferences and seminars sponsored by businesses and professional associations.

Experience in business is always an advantage. Experience in working with people in any way can give you confidence and develop important communication and interpersonal skills. Even if you have not worked part time or full time in a business, other types of experiences are useful. Working on projects in an organization, writing for the yearbook or school newspaper, forming a Junior Achievement company, or helping in a parent's business are all examples of experiences that can develop skills important in business.

Most employers value experience when they hire employees. It is relatively easy to find an entry-level job if you are not particularly concerned about the type of work or working conditions. These entry-level jobs provide the work experience that will qualify you for the jobs you prefer. Even though the pay may not be as high as you would like and work schedules are sometimes difficult to manage with school and extracurricular activities, it important to have a good work record in your first jobs.

Beginning employees who stay with one employer for a length of time and receive favorable evaluations will find it easier to receive promotions or be hired by an employer offering a better job. Employees who take advantage of training, opportunities for leadership, or the chance to supervise other employees or contribute to team activities will have an excellent employment record to use when applying for promotions or advanced jobs in other companies.

■ DEVELOPING A CAREER PLAN

Many people do little planning, even for the things that are most important to them. You know from your study of business that planning is an important skill. Businesses that plan are much more successful than those that do not plan. Likewise, people who plan their careers are more likely to achieve their career goals than those who do not plan. By developing a career plan, you will be able to practice an important business skill. In addition, you can show your plan to potential employers to demonstrate your ability to plan.

The following steps provide an outline to follow in developing a career plan:

1. *Develop an understanding of business concepts and the types of business careers.* Study careers in depth to determine the industries, businesses, and jobs that most interest you and the types of career paths related to those jobs.

ILLUSTRATION 25-5

Why is it wise to develop a career plan?

2. *Complete a self-assessment of your knowledge, skills, and attitudes that are related to those needed in business careers.* Ask a counselor to assist you with appropriate interest and aptitude tests that can help you with your assessment. Get feedback from people who know you well (family, friends, teachers, and employers) about their perceptions of the important skills, knowledge, and attitudes you have identified.

3. *Identify the education and experience requirements for business careers that interest you.* Compare those career requirements with your current preparation, and determine the additional education and experience you will need to qualify for those careers.

4. *Discuss the education and experience you will need with people (counselors or businesspeople) who are familiar with education programs and employment opportunities.* Have them help you select those that fit your career plans and qualifications.

5. *Develop a career plan that identifies the knowledge and skills needed for the career you have chosen and how you will develop them through a combination of education and experience.* The plan can identify the jobs in a career ladder, the schools or educational programs you plan to complete, how long you expect to take in moving through each step of the career ladder, and the ultimate career goal you would like to achieve.

■ PREPARING A CAREER PORTFOLIO

Artists, models, and advertising people have used portfolios for many years to demonstrate their abilities and present examples of their work. A **portfolio** is an organized collection of information and materials developed to represent yourself, your preparation, and your accomplishments. You might want to develop a portfolio to help you with

Exam4
?.2

career planning and to represent yourself when you apply for jobs or for admission to an educational institution.

Your portfolio should provide clear descriptions of your preparation, skills, and experience. Those descriptions can include examples of projects you have completed in school and on the job or for organizations to which you belong. They can even be work you have done as a hobby that demonstrates an important business skill. You can include in your portfolio evaluations of your skills and work evidenced through tests, checklists of competencies you have mastered, and performance reviews from employers. Also, you might ask people who know you well to write recommendations that relate to your skills and abilities.

You can develop your portfolio over a long period of time. You might start it now and continue to add to it as you complete high school, go on for additional education, or move through jobs in your career ladder. You should prepare a portfolio that allows you to add and remove items. Put your materials in a binder or other protective covering to keep them in good condition. The portfolio should include your best and most recent materials. Many people are now developing a personal Web site that includes their career portfolio. You can scan printed materials and photograph objects to add to your Internet portfolio. If you decide to use the Internet for this purpose, be careful to protect personal and confidential information.

A portfolio is a good way for you to identify important materials that will help you with your self-assessment. It also keeps materials organized so you can show them to others to demonstrate achievement, or as you apply for educational programs and jobs. Because it needs to communicate your preparation and skills effectively, it should be well organized, understandable, and easy for others to review.

CHAPTER CONCEPTS

■ The dramatic changes facing both traditional and new businesses present challenges to both employees and managers. Human resources personnel can help businesses respond to those changes by establishing organizational development programs.

■ Two important elements of an effective organizational development program are improving work processes and building effective working relationships. The goal is to make improvements to eliminate errors, improve quality, and reduce costs. Organizational development programs focus on management/employee relationships as well as relationships with people in other organizations with whom the company works and with the company's customers.

■ Successful businesses value their employees. They realize that it is not easy to find employees with the right qualifications and it can be very expensive to hire and train a new employee. Companies develop programs to increase employee motivation and performance, so they can retain an effective workforce.

■ Career development programs meet the company's future employment needs by systematically preparing current employees for future positions in the company. A successful career development program requires a long-term organizational plan, career paths, effective employee performance reviews, career counseling, and training and development for employees.

■ Companies depend on effective and satisfied employees. Those employees need up-to-date skills so they can perform their jobs accurately and efficiently. Two ways companies can contribute to maintaining a quality workforce are an effective system for performance review and well-designed training and development programs.

■ There are many opportunities for careers in business no matter what your interests, education, or experience. Careers paths exist in all types of businesses. International career opportunities are especially attractive to people who are well prepared for the special requirements of international business. Following career planning procedures will help you obtain a job that is both satisfying and rewarding.

BUILD VOCABULARY POWER

Define the following terms and concepts.

1. job security
2. organizational development
3. career development
4. customer service standards
5. performance standards
6. job design
7. job enlargement
8. cross training
9. job enrichment
10. career development program
11. career path

12. career plan
13. career centers
14. performance review
15. portfolio

REVIEW FACTS

1. What factor caused companies to make major changes in their organizational size, structure, and operations in the last part of the 20th century?
2. What are two important elements of effective organizational development?
3. In what ways can organizations make improvements in the way work is accomplished?
4. Identify factors in the external environment that are most likely to result in problems for organizations today.
5. What is the first step in planning and implementing an organizational development program?
6. Do most organizational development programs take a long or a short time to be successful?
7. What are four work factors that relate to increased employee satisfaction?
8. What is the difference between job enlargement and job enrichment?
9. Why do many businesses today view their employees as an important resource?
10. What are five components of an effective career development program?
11. How do performance reviews help employees make effective career decisions?
12. What are some examples of special career development programs?
13. Identify three guidelines that managers should follow in completing a performance review conference with an employee.
14. What are some situations that indicate a need for employee training?
15. In what ways can a portfolio help with career planning?

DISCUSS IDEAS

1. In what ways is the employment environment today different from the environment 10 years ago and in what ways is it similar?
2. Identify ways that the following levels of employees can most directly contribute to the success of a business: a beginning employee, an experienced employee, a supervisor, and the company's top executive or owner.
3. How can work processes be improved without changing the technology or equipment used to complete the work?
4. What are some valuable sources of information that managers can use to identify possible changes in the external environment?

5. What is the difference between a customer service standard and a performance standard? How can customer service standards influence performance standards?

6. The last step in developing and implementing an organizational development program is to make the new process part of the organization's culture. Why is that step important? Why do you believe it is often difficult to accomplish?

7. Using jobs with which you are familiar, suggest some ways organizations could use job enlargement and job enrichment to increase employee satisfaction and motivation.

8. What effect does employee morale have on productivity and absenteeism? Why do you think this is so?

9. What would be evidence that a company considers its employees to be a very important resource in achieving its goals? What would be evidence that the company does not value its employees?

10. Some companies believe that each employee should be totally responsible for his or her career development. Why is it likely that career development will not be successful in those companies?

11. Some of the best-performing companies also spend the most for employee training. Why would a successful company want to devote more time and money to training?

12. In what ways would planning for a career in international business be similar to or different from planning for a career in a person's home country?

13. What do you believe are the most important resources for career planning? Justify your answer.

ANALYZE INFORMATION

1. With the rest of your classmates, identify one problem related to the "work" environment or "work" relationships of your school. Then divide the class into several teams of students (4–6 students per group). Discuss the problem to identify why the problem exists and how the school would be better if the problem were solved. Then propose several solutions and analyze each to determine its advantages and disadvantages. Select the one solution your group believes could be implemented and that would be acceptable to administrators, teachers, and students. Prepare a written report from your group that identifies the problem, the proposed solution, and the key steps to successfully implementing the solution. Share your report with the other teams.

2. Conduct a survey of five people who have been working full time for more than three years. Ask them to identify the three things they like most and the three things they like least about their jobs. Combine your results with those of other class members. Organize the individual responses into similar categories so the

result is 4–6 categories for each of the two groups of responses. Develop a chart that illustrates the findings of the entire class. Participate in a class discussion to identify how organizations could use the information your class collected.

3. A review of a report on the amount of formal training activities of Yarcho and Slayton, Inc., revealed the following data:

Date of Training	Number of Participants	Cost of Training	Department
2-4	45	$ 900	Marketing
7-26	26	3,120	Information
1-13	11	495	Management
4-05	58	870	
9-29	32	960	Operations
5-30	65	3,250	
11-08	29	435	Accounting
3-19	12	900	and Finance
7-12	38	760	
12-01	19	855	

   a. Calculate the cost per participant of each training session.
   b. Determine the average cost of training per participant for the entire company.
   c. If Yarcho and Slayton has a total of 206 employees with 45 in Marketing, 58 in Information Management, 65 in Operations, and 38 in Accounting and Finance, determine the average amount spent on each employee for training for each department and for the entire company.

4. Obtain a copy of an employee evaluation form from a business or use one provided by your teacher. Fill it out as if you were the supervisor or manager of an employee. Make sure to identify both areas where the employee performs well and a few areas for improvement. Then use the form to role-play a performance review conference with another student in your class. Have a third student observe the conference. That student should make notes on the responses and reactions of the two students engaged in the role-play. When you have completed the role-play, participate in a discussion with the other two team members, noting what appeared to work well and how the conference could be improved. After the discussion, form another team and repeat the process until each student has completed each role.

5. Identify the title of a management job that interests you. Using career information from your school counseling center, a library, or the Internet, prepare a description of the education and experience requirements for the job. Now search the career information to identify an entry-level job and at least two other related jobs that have increasing requirements and responsibilities and

could form a career path for you if you wanted to obtain the management job. Write a complete job description for each of the jobs. Now begin to develop a career portfolio for the career path by developing clear descriptions of your relevant preparation, skills, and experiences. Identify projects or other materials you have developed in this class or from other sources that would make useful additions to your portfolio. Identify the skills, including interpersonal skills, that you need to develop to progress along the career path. Research opportunities for professional self-improvement and life-long learning that will help you gain these skills.

SOLVE BUSINESS PROBLEMS

CASE 25-1

The Orion Corporation recently implemented employee involvement teams as a part of an organizational development program. The employees in the customer support department of the engineering division were excited about the chance to participate in solving a problem they had been facing for some time. Fourteen of the twenty employees had school-aged children. Several times during the year, the employees needed to take time from work to attend parent-teacher conferences, help with projects in their child's school, or attend an important school activity involving their children. Orion had no policy that allowed employees time away from work. The employees either had to miss the school activities or call in sick. Most of the employees felt uncomfortable about taking a "sick-day" when they really were not sick.

The employee team worked carefully and developed the following plan: Each employee could have up to two half-day absences for school-related activities during the year. The absence would have to be scheduled at least one week in advance and only one employee could be absent at a time. The other employees agreed to complete the work of the absent employee before they left for the day without additional pay. The department manager could cancel the absence with one day's notice if the department had special assignments or extra work.

The employee team submitted their plan to the department manager. The manager rejected the employee recommendation. She identified two reasons for rejecting the plan: (1) The company could not have different policies concerning employee absences for each department. (2) Since all employees in the department did not have school-aged children, the policy would be unfair to those employees.

Think Critically:

1. Do you believe the manager made the right decision about the team's recommendation? Why or why not? If you were the manager, how would you respond to the team's recommendation?
2. How do you believe the employees will feel about the organization, based on the manager's response to their proposal? What should the manager do now, based on her decision not to accept the team's recommendation?
3. How could the Orion Corporation improve the way it organized and used teams in the future?

CASE 25-2

Jacki Knox had just left her workstation when her supervisor, Dorothea Fernandez, stopped her.

Dorothea: *Do you have a few minutes, Jacki? I'd like to go over your performance evaluation with you.*

Jacki: *I'm just ready to go on break.*

Dorothea: *That's where I'm going, too. Let's get a table together in the break room and review your evaluation form. It shouldn't take very long.*

After they found a table in the corner of the break room, Dorothea removed an evaluation form from the folder she was carrying and handed it to Jacki.

Dorothea: *I think you're doing a very good job, Jacki. Your ratings have gone from four to five in three categories, and that's the top rating. You have maintained fours in four other categories. You need to pay attention to the two categories where I gave you a three and really work on the area where you received only a two. You're really a nice person, Jacki, and I'm happy to have you in my department. Do you have any questions?*

Jacki: *Well, I haven't had a chance to study the form, so I am not sure about questions. I'm obviously concerned about the areas where I received low ratings. Is this my formal evaluation that will determine if I get a salary increase?*

Dorothea: *No. We'll complete that in four more weeks. I just wanted you to see the form informally so we could discuss your performance before you had the formal evaluation.*

Just then a receptionist came to the table and told Dorothea that she had a visitor in her department.

Dorothea: *Jacki, why don't you spend some time reviewing the evaluation? Then we'll schedule some time in my office to discuss it completely.*

Think Critically:

1. Analyze the procedures Dorothea followed in discussing Jacki's evaluation with her. What were Dorothea's strengths and weaknesses?
2. Describe what Dorothea should do to improve the conference when she and Jacki meet again.
3. What should Jacki do to prepare for the next meeting with Dorothea? How should Jacki use the information she received from Dorothea and from the evaluation form during the next four weeks?

PROJECT: MY BUSINESS, INC.

Even new businesses must be concerned about change and maintaining an effective work environment and work processes. One of the serious problems faced by small businesses is being able to develop the skills of employees and then encourage them to continue to work for the business rather than changing jobs. The following activities will help you consider how to maintain an effective organization and develop effective, motivated employees.

DATA COLLECTION

1. Review magazine and newspaper articles about small business operations. Identify the types of problems small businesses face that often lead to major problems or failure of the business.

2. Identify a small number of people who have worked in a small business for a short time and then changed jobs due to dissatisfaction with the job. Also identify a small number who have worked in a small business and are satisfied with their jobs. Ask each group the reasons for their satisfaction or dissatisfaction. Ask them to identify which of the reasons are directly related to the size of the business and which are not related to the business's size.

3. Go to the Internet and gather information on the type of employee training that is currently being provided to employees by retail businesses. If possible, identify the amount of money small businesses spend on average to train employees compared to the amount spent by large businesses.

4. Identify the interpersonal skills you will need to develop as the manager of a small business. Gather information from the library or Internet about opportunities for professional self-improvement and life-long learning that could help you improve your skills as a business owner.

ANALYSIS

1. Prepare an outline of the training you would provide to each new employee of your business. Identify the training methods you would use, the materials or resources you would need, and the amount of time you would spend in training.

2. Develop a form to be used in reviewing the performance of your employees. Then outline the procedures you would follow to evaluate each employee's performance and to review the results of the evaluation with the employee.

3. Compile a list of things you could do as the owner of a new small business to develop a work environment that would be motivating for employees while encouraging effective performance. Try to list things that would not be particularly expensive to implement.

4. Assume that your business has been receiving an increased number of customer complaints. When you question your employees, they tell you that they are unsure of how to deal with difficult customers. Identify employee attitudes that result in customer satisfaction. Develop a procedure your employees could use in complex situations, including follow-up techniques.